My
TAPESTRY

Experiencing the Love of the Designer

Annette Batterink

MY TAPESTRY
Copyright © 2017 by Annette Batterink

For more information on Annette Batterink, go to:
https://mytapestryblog.wordpress.com/.

Printed in Canada

ISBN: 978-1-4866-1426-4

Word Alive Press
131 Cordite Road, Winnipeg, MB R3W 1S1
www.wordalivepress.ca

Library and Archives Canada Cataloguing in Publication

Batterink, Annette, author
    My tapestry : experiencing the love of the designer / Annette Batterink.

Issued in print and electronic formats.
ISBN 978-1-4866-1426-4 (softcover).--ISBN 978-1-4866-1427-1 (ebook)

    1. Batterink, Annette. 2. Christian biography--Canada. I. Title.

BR1725.B38A3 2017   277.1'083092   C2017-900200-7
                                                 C2017-900201-5

All the days ordained for me were written in your book before one of them came to be.

—Psalm 139:16

CONTENTS

FOR MY PARENTS— WITH THANKS TO GOD!

During World War II, my parents lived in the Netherlands, which was occupied by Nazi Germany. It was a very difficult time, and hard choices had to be made. Near the end of the war, my parents were engaged and working in the Wieringermeer polder, which was low-lying land reclaimed from the sea. Dikes and pumping engines kept the land dry.

In the beginning of 1945, under German command, Dutch workers dug deep holes at the bottom and at the top of the dikes. Each hole was loaded with unexploded bombs from British and American aircraft. On April 17, 1945, at 12:15 a.m. the explosives were ignited. The seven thousand people who lived in the Wieringermeer and the estimated one to two thousand refugees had to leave the polder. Within forty-eight hours the entire polder was filled with water. The people living there had been warned, and there was no loss of life.

On April 22, 1945, my father, then twenty-four years old, wrote in his diary that he and my mother went to look at the polder from part of the dike. He wrote, "It was a sorry sight—water all over with here and there a rooftop and tree showing. If we didn't know God cares for us, we would be devastated…The Lord is right in all His ways and works."

After my father died, my brother Len wrote *Afterword*—the final words about Dad's life—as an ending to my father's autobiography, *A Life of Grace and Blessings*. Len wrote, "In his book, Dad talked about his engagement to Mom years before. He said, 'We loved each other dearly.'

For sixty-two and a half years their love for each other grew stronger and deeper. It was at the heart of the family, and it blessed everyone they knew."

My parents' example of trust in God and their love for each other greatly shaped my life. I thank God for the parents He gave me and for the example they were to me and my children. I dedicate this book to the many special memories of my parents.

INTRODUCTION

The threads of the tapestry of my life started long before I was born and go on into eternity. Through brilliant colours and dark hues, knots and zigzag lines, God is creating a picture that only He could design. In the Weaver's design, there are no mistakes. There are threads that remind me that God was preparing me for the tough times before they even happened; threads filled with pain that still bring tears to my eyes; threads that bring back memories that make me smile and bring joy to my day. Parts of the tapestry seem complete, and parts are still being woven into surprising patterns. The Weaver loves me, and I trust Him more and more.

On Sunday, February 8, 1998, I was living in Ontario. Bob, my husband, rented a U-Haul trailer and announced to my children and me that he was moving to Alberta. It was a pivotal moment in my life in that I began to understand that it was time to allow God to do a new thing in my life, to cleanse me and renew me. I had gotten lost and confused, tired and despairing. It was the beginning of an ongoing journey of learning to love myself. Outward changes didn't happen immediately, but deep inside I was different.

I thought for a long time about writing my life story "someday." Part of me became stuck in the past, waiting for the day when I would start writing. The experience of writing about events before and after that day in 1998 has been cathartic. God helped me see wonders in the threads from my past that could only be by His design. These are my experiences, and I've related them honestly to the best of my ability. For various reasons, I've made attempts to protect the identity of some people.

———

Our journey with Christ is not intended to be a striving to attain something we are not, but to become who we are! Like the butterfly, God has already placed inside you everything He wants you to be.[1]

———

1 Dutch Sheets, *Becoming Who You Are* [Bloomington, Minnesota: Bethany House Publishers, 2010], 15

chapter one
BEFORE ME

The LORD had said to Abram, "Go from your country, your people and your father's household to the land I will show you."

—Genesis 12:1

MY FAVOURITE MEMORIES OF DAD ARE THE TIMES WHEN HE OR I WOULD SAY something silly and we would give each other "the look." For me, it was loving communication at its best. My father was born in the Netherlands in the early 1920s, the eldest of a set of twins, with twin brothers and a much younger sister. When his school years ended, at the age of thirteen he had to decide what he wanted to do with his life. He had hoped to become a minister, but that was "too expensive." He told his father that he wanted to work with something alive. He decided to become a farmer and work with seeds and animals, and he left home to work on an uncle's farm.

While still a youth, my father became friends with a young man, Ralph, whose family lived on a farm. When Dad visited the family, his friend's studious youngest sister caught his eye. She would one day become my mother: young love, first love, only love.

A treasured memory of my mother is when she was already experiencing some symptoms of dementia. Mom was asleep the evening that Dad died, so the decision was made to tell her about Dad's death after she woke up. I stayed in their room that night. Early in the morning, after I told Mom that Dad had died, she asked me to crawl into her nursing home bed with her. As we cuddled together, she would talk a little, pat my cheek and tell me how wonderful her children were, and then repeat the same actions. After a while she told me I'd better leave and get some more sleep. I could soon hear her gentle snores.

My mother was also born in the Netherlands in the early 1920s. She had three brothers and four sisters. Because she had older sisters at home, Mom was able to go to school longer than my father had. Mom learned some English, but she especially like math and hoped to become a teacher. Her plans ended when World War II started.

My parents' relationship grew deeper and stronger during the years of the war, first through correspondence and later when they both worked in the Wieringermeer polder. When the war was over, they figured out how to bike past areas that had been damaged by the Germans and return to their parents' homes. Their next challenge was to find jobs and housing in their war-torn country, as they hoped to get married. God provided, and they got married on June 14, 1946.

My parents were able to find a chicken coop, which they converted into a living space. An aunt told me years later that the chicken coop had been a cozy living space. Sadness soon came into my parents' lives. My mother had complications at the end of her first pregnancy and delivered a stillborn son on my parents' first wedding anniversary. It was an event that they seldom talked about. There was much rejoicing more than two years later when my sister Mary was born.

My father had attended agricultural college, but there was no farmland available. Because of the lack of opportunities in the Netherlands, many families emigrated to various countries. Two of my mother's brothers, Klaas and Ralph, had already left for Canada with their families, and my parents soon made plans to follow. A farmer sponsored my parents, and Dad would work for him initially. I once asked my father if he came to Canada so there would be more opportunities for his children. He said, "I'm not as selfless as that. I wanted more opportunities for myself, too."

In the beginning of 1952, my parents were notified that they would have passage on a ship called the *Rijndam*. On April 17, 1952, when my sister was two and a half years old, the young family of three left everything familiar and set sail for a new country. Before leaving the Netherlands, my parents noticed that the name of the sponsor on their visa and passport was different than the name they had been given earlier. They wanted to live close to my mother's youngest brother, Uncle Ralph, in southwestern Ontario, near Forest. The name on their documents was of someone who lived in eastern Ontario, near Napanee. They were told that the confusion would be straightened out by the "fieldman" when they got to Canada. (In the years after World War II, when many immigrants came to Canada, the Christian Reformed Church appointed fieldmen in certain areas of Canada. These men were an English-speaking contact for newly arrived immigrants.)

The *Rijndam* docked at Pier 21 in Halifax, where many Dutch immigrants first stepped on Canadian soil. Immediately, my parents had a difficult decision to make. Changing sponsorship didn't seem to be possible. My father wrote in his autobiography, "The fieldman told us that if we went on we would never be able to become Canadians and we would have a bad name and would not be able to get credit at the bank." (None of the threats proved to be true.) My parents insisted on living closer to family, so they moved on to southwestern Ontario without support, trusting God with their future.

My parents and sister went to stay with my Uncle Ralph and his family until they could find another farmer to work for. After a few short-term jobs, they found a more permanent position with a farmer who lived east of Sarnia. My father worked on the farm, and my mother helped in the house. Though further away from family than they had planned, it was good to have steady work. My parents met Charlie and Lee Huizinga, who drove them to church in Sarnia. The friendship that was formed lasted a lifetime for my parents and our family.

About a year later, Dad and Mom had an opportunity to live in their desired location. On Dallas McColl's farm, they lived in a garage that had been converted into an apartment for them. It wasn't long before Uncle Ralph and his family moved away. However, by that time, my parents were part of the Forest Christian Reformed church family, and great friendships were being formed. With many challenges, changes, and blessings, their life in their new country had started.

chapter two

THE FOREST YEARS

Whoever fears the LORD *has a secure fortress, and for their children it will be a refuge.*

—Proverbs 14:26

IN THE SNOWY EARLY MORNING HOURS OF SUNDAY, FEBRUARY 14, 1954, I WAS born in Sarnia General Hospital. I was the tiniest of my parents' babies even though they later had a set of twins. My sister, Mary, was four and a half years old when I arrived, so I'm quite sure I didn't lack for attention. I was named Hilda Annette after my maternal grandparents.

I was called Hilda for the first twelve years of my life. Just before my twelfth birthday, I asked my parents if I could start using my second name, Annette. A few days later, my teacher was returning test papers and asked, "Who here is Annette?" I think he was a bit frustrated by the change for a few days, but the adjustment was made quite easily by him, by my classmates, and by my family.

On the morning of my birth, because of the snow and his lack of sleep, Dad decided to drop in on Charlie and Lee Huizinga, who now lived in Sarnia. Charlie would jokingly remind me often through the years about how I had made him get up early on the day I was born. One of those reminders was at Dad and Mom's fortieth wedding anniversary celebration. Charlie read, "Then Annette was born. Did we ever feel that! Very early in the morning one day in February, we woke up because someone threw stones at our bedroom window."

My first home was the garage apartment on Dallas McColl's farm. Dad wrote in his autobiography, "I think Mr. McColl was a bit jealous for they had only boys and we now had two girls." Years later, when I was working at a hospital, Dallas was one of my patients, and I met his wife and daughter. We soon realized the connection between us. At home that evening, I reread the segment in Dad's book about the McColl family. I had a chance to tell their daughter what I'd read about my father thinking that her father was a bit jealous. She surprised me by saying, "So *you* are the reason why my parents adopted me!" It was a sweet moment and a colourful thread in my tapestry.

My next home was in a farmhouse when Dad started working for a turkey farmer. The house had no indoor plumbing except for a pump in the pantry. Wood needed to be readily available in the large wood box as woodstoves were used for much of the cooking and heat. Mary and I soon discovered that the wood box was the best hiding place in the house. Dad always had trouble finding us there. We didn't realize that for Dad, the problem wasn't that he didn't know where we were; it was pretending that his smart girls had once again found the best hiding place. Dad loved his girls.

My twin brothers, Leonard (Len) and Clarence, were born on May 2, 1956. It was a difficult delivery for my mother, and she spent a few weeks in the hospital. While she was there, Mary and I stayed with the Doornbosch family. Mary was very clingy with Mom after she came home as she had been very homesick.

The twins took a lot of time and attention. All the water for washing people and clothes had to be pumped into buckets and heated on the woodstove. Jenny Van Dyk, who lived nearby, and other women came to help in the home. In January of 1957, Mom had a hysterectomy, which meant more disruption in the family routine.

My world changed a lot when my brothers were born. I had been the centre of attention, and now I felt deserted. In most of my very early memories I am by myself. Mom wasn't feeling well, and my sister wasn't my usual happy playmate. Sadly, though no one did anything wrong, a root of rejection was planted, a seed that germinated for a long time.

In my late teens, I began to struggle with feeling like I couldn't measure up to my parents' expectations of me. Years later, when healing came into my life, I recognized that the enemy is a liar. My sister, Mary, remembers that when my parents went to the store to buy her a bicycle, they bought me a tricycle. I walked up to a tricycle in the store and said, "I finally found my bike." My parents, immigrants with little money, bought the tricycle, too. I have a photograph of three-year-old me sitting on my tricycle with a huge smile on my face. I had tangible proof of my parents' generosity towards me. They had a season of busyness, but I had not been rejected.

Also when I was three, I fell out of the back seat of the car onto Highway 7 north of Toronto. I had opened the back door, which apparently wasn't hard to do in those old cars, and was rolling down the highway. My father wrote in his book, "She was all scratched up and cried loudly, so she was good and alive. We cleaned her up as well as we could and went on." It was many years later when I noticed that part of my outer left ear is missing. God's angels had been protecting me from further harm that day. His purposes for me were not completed.

In mid-December 1958, my parents celebrated twelve and a half years of marriage, which is a Dutch custom. As a gift, my parents got a reel-to-reel tape from their siblings in the Netherlands. They borrowed the tape player that belonged to the church and invited their friends from church to join them. There was much fun and laughter as they listened to the greetings and stories from our Dutch relatives in the Dutch language.

Our church family became important people in my life due to strong bonds among immigrants in the Dutch Christian Reformed community. In many ways they replaced the uncles and aunts who couldn't be a part of my life.

The threads of my tapestry zig and zag and interconnect at unexpected times and in unexpected places, often making it fun to play Dutch Bingo. *The Urban Dictionary* describes Dutch Bingo this way: "A game that many Dutchmen play when trying to figure out how they know each other, and/or how they probably are related!" There have been too many surprising connections to mention, but each one reminds me of God's faithfulness through the years of my life.

In the spring of 1959, my parents bought their own fifty-acre farm for $6,000. We still went to Forest for shopping and church. The best part of moving to the new house was the indoor plumbing: a flush toilet and a bathtub. On his farm, Dad was able to plant his own seeds and tend his own animals. It was a dream come true, even though Dad needed to work off of the farm as well to earn more money. The house needed paint, the barn needed repairs, and some small building needed to be torn down, but it was a beginning. Pigpens were built, and later, with the help of Oom Klaas and cousins, the barn was prepared for baby chicks. The house was painted white with green trim. Even as a child, I enjoyed seeing the changes.

Life on the farm was a lot of work for my parents, but it was a fun place for me. It was very dark outside at night unless there was a full moon, as there were no street lights. I discovered that if I looked outside when the moon was full, the whole world was lit up with a glorious glow that changed everything into a black-and-white photograph.

On a warm summer evening, the Huizinga family from Sarnia came for a visit. We young ones were all lying on the grass watching for shooting stars. There were too many stars to count. We could hear our parents visiting in the house and the frogs croaking by the pond. All was peaceful and calm and right with the world. I can still feel the coolness of the grass underneath my arms and feet.

I grew up being taught that God reveals Himself through His Word and through nature. Mary had learned the names of many different birds, trees and flowers, and she was very willing to teach me everything she knew. I was amazed watching the hummingbirds drink the nectar from flowers and seeing redwing blackbirds among the bulrushes and colourful Baltimore orioles swooping over the pasture. I experienced the wonder of piglets and calves being born. Perhaps it was during those times that Mary and I began to notice God in the ordinary things of life. It has been a blessing to notice little "God-touches" and share them with her all through the years.

———

Some winter evenings, Dad and Mary attended functions at church and I was allowed to stay up late with Mom. I was fascinated watching Mom knit and read a book at the same time. I would have helped Mom prepare the yarn earlier. To save money, she unravelled knitted sweaters and knit something new with the yarn. While she unravelled, I wound the yarn around a wooden board. Mom would steam the yarn, and when it was dry, I rolled the yarn into balls. My mother wasn't a difficult taskmaster. It was good to learn that helping someone can often be an enjoyable experience and that working together gets the job done quickly.

My father taught us that Sunday, a day of rest, was a gift to be appreciated and honoured. We attended church services twice during the day, and the remaining hours were our chance to relax from our normal routine. During high school, it was great to take a day off from studying and doing homework, especially during exam week. I think I was able to function better the rest of the week after taking a break. In later years, it was a challenge to take a day off when I worked shifts and had to work on Sundays. I learned that rest is not just a gift; it's a necessity.

———

On August 23, 1960, Dad had an industrial accident. He worked in a brick-making factory, and one of the prongs used to make holes in a concrete block went through his wrist. It was his left wrist, and he was left-handed. There was extensive damage, but the hand was spared. My mother called our pastor, Rev. Cooper, after she got the phone call. He came to the farm to take all of us to the Sarnia hospital where Dad was. Children were not allowed into the hospital to visit in those days, so we had to wait in the car.

On subsequent visits, my mother found the best place to park the car along the tree-lined street, and my three siblings and I waited in the car while she visited Dad. On one special Sunday afternoon, we were allowed into the waiting room inside the doors of the hospital. Dad came down from his room, and it was so good to see him! He had a cast on his arm, but his smile was still the same. He was still Dad!

A picture of Mary and me on my first day of school, in September 1960, shows Dad in the background with a cast. I was excited about going to school. I had recently met Dad's cousin's daughter Helen, and I knew she would be in my class. Helen became my best friend, and our friendship spanned many years. Mary started grade 7 when I started grade 1. She had taught me more than I would have learned if I had attended kindergarten, so I was disappointed not to be given a book to read on my first day of classes. We attended a two-room Christian school in Wyoming, Ontario, with four grades in each classroom. One of the people in my classroom was a girl named Ellie, and her "thread" reappeared in my tapestry through the years.

The first winter after Dad's accident, he spent weekdays in the Workmen's Compensation Hospital in Toronto for rehabilitation, and he returned home on weekends. It was a very busy time on the farm. Lots of pigs had piglets, and more pigpens had to be built. Mom's cousin and his wife came to help, but it must have been a very challenging time for my mother. She was caring for her four young children, ages four to eleven, along with tending to the needs of the farm.

God made it evident through our neighbours that He was watching over us. Our crank telephone was on a party line. If we wanted to make a call, we had to check to see if the line was already in use. If another subscriber was on the line, we could hear them and participate in their conversation if we wanted to. There was a clicking noise when another person came on the line, so eavesdroppers were noticed.

One Friday evening a neighbour on our telephone party line listened in on a call when my father called my mother. The neighbour knew our family's situation well enough to guess why our phone rang at that time of the evening. It was a snowy winter evening when Dad was coming home from Toronto, and Mom had to pick him up from the train station. After listening long enough to be sure my father needed to be picked up, the neighbour interrupted the conversation and volunteered to go get Dad. The offer was accepted and greatly appreciated.

———

In the spring of grade 1, I wasn't feeling well. I ached, and I cried because of the pain. After a doctor's visit, further tests needed to be done. In his autobiography, my father wrote, "We had to go with her to Sarnia Hospital for blood tests. She didn't like that at all and screamed from beginning to end. You could hear her about two blocks away." Blood test results showed that I had rheumatic fever, probably following a strep throat. Rheumatic fever is an autoimmune disease, and some theories say that stress can be a contributing influence in autoimmune disorders. Perhaps "little me" was more affected by events at home than any of us realized.

Besides the joint pains I was experiencing, rheumatic fever can be damaging to the heart. Therefore I was placed on complete bed rest. I had to take aspirin and penicillin every day for a few years. It was fortunate that my parents decided to take care of me at home rather than have me hospitalized. While I was on complete bed rest, my parents had to carry me everywhere: to the bathroom, to bed, outside to sit. I spent most of my days on a couch in the dining room, which was where most of our family activities happened. When the weather was warm enough, I was placed on a lawn chair outside. Sometimes the wind blew, dark clouds rolled in, and I could see the underside of the leaves on the trees. I knew a thunderstorm was approaching quickly—and I'd just wait for a parent to come to carry me inside.

One day my teacher came to visit me after school. I got *Highlights* magazines and books to read. When friends came to visit, they played with me for a while, but soon they joined in the fun my siblings were having. I can still picture everyone running out of the room going to "somewhere." The need to stay in bed must have been clearly explained to me. Through those waiting-alone times, I was learning valuable lessons that God would use later in my life.

One day was tougher, though. There was lots of excitement on our farm when our first baby chicks arrived. I had to wait until my father had time to carry me to the barn before I could see them. They were adorable balls of yellow fluff, less than one day old. They were kept safe inside a brooder, which on our farm was a circle of corrugated cardboard with a brooder lamp for warmth above the centre. My father had to check his precious chicks several times a day those first days, and he had the patience to carry me along a few more times.

I don't remember being totally frustrated with being on bedrest. I must have been able to keep myself entertained with quiet things. After some time, I was allowed up for an hour a day. Sometimes Mom got distracted talking on the telephone and I had some extra time of "freedom." I wasn't allowed strenuous activity for a long time. For the next two years I missed physical education classes and had to stay in at recess time if the weather was damp or cold.

———

During my first two years of school, Mary and I had been picked up by car and taken to a bus that went to our school. When Mary began attending high school, my brothers started going to school with me. More children from the Forest community were enrolled, and a local bus was needed. My father became the bus driver. With all of her children in school, my mother started doing some work outside the home. She did cleaning in the home of one of the neighbours, and our after-school routine changed on those days. In my parents' home, there were regular mealtimes and break times. Devotions at mealtimes were also part of the routine. The highlight for many years was teatime. Whenever possible, we would sit down with Mom after school and have tea and a snack. I especially appreciated that routine as I got older. It was good to have those times of sharing my day.

———

At the end of grade 2, my teacher wrote in my report card, "She has been able to do grade 3 work easily. With help this summer I think she should be able to do grade 4 work in the fall." It was an adjustment being in a different grade than all my friends, even though we were in the same classroom. My desk was in a row that had grade 3 students in front of me and grade 4 students behind me. Staying in for recess the many times I had to because of the weather didn't seem so bad that year. It was a confusing year. I wasn't quite sure where I belonged. Perhaps this was a preparation time for more changes that were coming before the next school year.

Two months into grade 4, in October 1962, a scary event happened. In later years I remembered the fear but not the event that caused it. By searching using Google, I discovered that it was the Cuban missile crisis. On October 14, 1962, a US Air Force U-2 spy plane captured photos of a medium-range ballistic missile site under construction near San Cristobal on the island of Cuba. There was no doubt that the construction materials and the missiles were Soviet in origin. For the thirty-seven days that followed that October day, the world teetered on the edge of nuclear annihilation.

One of the older boys in my class made me very afraid that our country would soon be at war. He told me that even boys from the school would have to fight. One evening my mother sat on the side of my bed and calmed my fears and prayed with me. She had lived through a world war, had stood on a dike near a flooded polder, and had still trusted God's care for her. She was able to speak peace to me. Years later when our family celebrated Mom's 80th birthday, we shared memories of her. I was surprised when I was overcome with emotion as I tried to tell everyone about the blessing Mom had been to me on that evening in 1962.

When we lived on the turkey farm my parents bought a piano. First Mary took piano lessons, and later I had some too. During Mary's teen years, she and I would sometimes sing hymns together around the piano, all the verses of many songs. One dark night when our family was travelling down a highway, Mary and I sang for almost two hours in the back of the car. We sang one hymn after another until we couldn't think of any more that we had memorized. Many of those words are still deeply rooted in my heart.

From 1963 to 1968, I was a member of the Bible Reader's League, started by "Uncle Bill." I had an opportunity to join through the Christian school I attended. Uncle Bill sent me $1 after I completed one year of daily Bible reading, $2 after two years and $5 when I completed five years. In a letter written on February 4, 1968, Uncle Bill wrote,

> You have successfully completed the five-year course of our B. R. L. Congratulations!…It is my prayer that He may keep you close to His loving heart and guide you all the way every day, as by His hand, through all your life. I hope that the habit of your daily personal, private devotions may be established firmly as an individual part of your daily routine.

I am thankful that Bill Uitvlugt, a Christian school principal in a school in eastern Ontario, started a club that I was able to join. Uncle Bill's prayer is still being answered.

———

For three years after his injury, Dad struggled to do all the work on the farm. Because of chronic pain and the limited use of his left hand, it was too difficult. Dad had to give up his lifelong dream, and we had to leave the farm. It must have been a hard time for my father, but I don't remember him showing any anger or bitterness. It was many years before he found a job that suited him well in his changed circumstances. One of Dad's favourite verses was the following:

> *"Two things I ask of you, LORD; do not refuse me before I die: Keep falsehood and lies far from me; give me neither poverty nor riches, but give me only my daily bread. Otherwise, I may have too much and disown you and say 'Who is the LORD?' Or I may become poor and steal, and so dishonor the name of my God."*
>
> —Proverbs 30:7–9

During the early years of my life there were many lessons and blessings. I was surrounded by an awesome variety of sights, sounds, and smells of God's creation. I became aware of the circle of life—birth, growth, reproduction, and death. I learned to appreciate the family of God, as we were part of a small, loving, caring church community that became part of our social life as well. My illness made me adapt in ways that were perhaps unexpected for a young child. And lastly, my father accepted the needed changes when his injury altered the course of his life. I thank God for His care and provision.

chapter three

THE SARNIA YEARS

So that your trust may be in the LORD, I teach you today, even you.
—Proverbs 22:19

WHEN I WAS NINE YEARS OLD, OUR FAMILY MOVED FROM THE COUNTRY INTO the city of Sarnia, Ontario, so Dad could pursue different job opportunities. Through an exchange arrangement, a young family moved to our farm and we moved to their home in the city. It was a huge change for us. Chemical Valley, a complex of oil refining and chemical companies, was south of the city. Some days we smelled the awful oily smells and could taste the air. Sarnia is on the shores of Lake Huron and the St. Clair River, which are part of the Great Lakes St. Lawrence Seaway System. On foggy nights, when the seaway was open, we could hear the foghorns from the big "lakers" (bulk carriers) as they navigated through the fog. These smells and sounds were very different from those on our farm.

Our new home was on a tree-lined street in the centre of the city. There was very little space between our house and the neighbours' house on one side and only a single driveway between our house and the house on the other side. It always seemed dark and dreary in that house. When light shone in my bedroom window at night, it wasn't from the moon; it was from a bedroom in the house next door. When my seven-year-old brothers and I were outside, my mother had to frequently remind us not to be so noisy. I was happy that there was a park a few blocks away where we could run and shout and use our imaginations to our hearts' content.

The playground had a piece of equipment shaped like a rocket. We had many adventures on that rocket. We lived in the years of the space race between the United States and the Soviet Union, and I was in grade 2 when John Glenn made three orbits around the earth in 1962. There were many more spaceflights as each country tried to be first to get a man on the moon. On July 20, 1969, American men landed on the moon for the first time. First we heard Neil Armstrong say, "The *Eagle* has landed" when the lunar aircraft landed on the moon. Later, he said, "That's one small step for man, one giant leap for mankind" as he took his first step on to the lunar surface.

Many years later, on the clear, crisp evening of December 20, 2006, between 6:15 and 6:25, I first saw the space shuttle *Discovery* and then the International Space Station (ISS) as they orbited overhead. The ISS is a habitable artificial satellite in low-Earth orbit. The space shuttle was a crewed partially reusable low-Earth orbital spacecraft. Several years later, when Canadian Chris Hatfield was in the ISS, I was living in BC. I was excited again when I spotted the ISS moving across the morning sky. I realized that the wonders of space travel are exciting but not awe-inspiring like a starry night sky.

———

After our move to Sarnia, it wasn't too difficult for me to adjust to a new Christian school, even though there were so many more students. There were two familiar people right from the start. My grade 5 teacher had been my grade 1 teacher at the other school, and the Huizingas' son was in my class. I soon felt accepted and enjoyed going to school. I had a few best friends while at that school but never one special friend like Helen had been.

My mother was soon cleaning houses a day or two a week. During summer vacation, when Mary had a summer job, I was left in charge of my brothers. We weren't allowed to venture too far from home when Mom wasn't there. The days were brightened up a bit by the flickering of the TV when we watched reruns of *I Love Lucy* and probably some game shows too. It was boring and not much fun. I haven't thought of it often over the years, but I imagine that my mother felt as challenged by those circumstances as I did later when I had to work when my children were at home.

On Friday, November 22, 1963, US President John F. Kennedy was as-sassinated as he rode in a motorcade in Dallas, Texas. My grade 5 class was told the news just before our afternoon recess. It was shocking news! My girlfriends and I wandered aimlessly around the playground as we talked about something we couldn't fully understand. My family and I watched TV for much of that weekend as the story continued to unfold. On Sunday, November 24, we watched as Jack Ruby fatally shot Lee Harvey Oswald in the abdomen, live on TV. As an adult, it's hard for me to imagine that I was a nine-year-old child as those events unfolded.

The mid-1960s were the days of penny candy, six NHL teams, and the Beatles. Three variety stores in close vicinity had lots of different candy to choose from. It was worthwhile to hunt for pop bottles in that neighbourhood—the glass ones, of course! And the Beatles were *big* news. I was fascinated watching the mass hysteria at their debut US performance on the *Ed Sullivan Show*. I soon knew all the words to most of the Beatles' songs, and their "mop-top" haircuts became as popular as their songs.

We had good neighbours in the city as well. No matter where my parents lived, they got along well with their neighbours. The family right next door had a cottage at Miller Lake on the Bruce Peninsula. Even after we no longer lived in the neighbourhood, my parents, brothers, and I stayed at their cottage for a week. In later years I returned to Miller Lake several times, always when Mary and her family were there, sometimes with my family, and sometimes alone.

After two year of inner-city living, our family moved to Sarnia Township, near the local Christian school and our church. Dad was working in real estate at the time and found a house that was bright, airy, and also room-ier. During the years we lived there I did lots and lots and lots of reading and could always find a private spot where I could curl up with a book.

Our yard there was much larger. Sometimes I cut the grass because I wanted to. Slow and steady got the job done. Dad teasingly commented that he didn't usually have to add extra gas when *he* cut the grass. In our large garden, my father could once again plant seeds and watch things grow: vegetables, strawberries, and raspberries. In the summer, my brothers and I helped Mom prepare food from the garden or a fruit farm for the freezer or for canning. I gained skills that brought me pleasure when I had my own home.

There was also time for fun and freedom. We lived on the edge of the city, near open fields and within biking distance of creeks and ponds. There were lots of children in our neighbourhood, so there was always someone to go exploring with. The field at the end of our street was a wide open space with a few trees. In the summer grasses were so tall that a person could hide there and not be seen. It was in that field, crouching in the grass, that I had my first and last cigarette.

In 1966, because my father still always had pain in his left wrist, he had surgery to have his wrist fused, and he was no longer able to move it. Dad was not allowed to work for several weeks after the surgery, so my parents decided to take the opportunity to go back to the Netherlands for first time since their immigration fourteen years earlier. For many years I had watched my mother eagerly look for airmail letters in the mailbox. It must have been a joyous reunion to see all those people again!

Canada's centennial year, 1967, was my graduating year from elementary school, which was grade 8 in Ontario. Our class had fifty students that year, two classes of twenty-five students. On May 9, 1967, all the students plus some teachers, parents and school board members travelled by train to Toronto. We attended a half-hour session of the Ontario government in action and then toured the Ontario legislative buildings. The train and subway rides were the most memorable part of the day for me. It was a great, fun adventure, a worthy way of celebrating Canada's 100th birthday. There was a lot of pride in our country that year, and I still have a scrapbook I made. In 2017, it will be Canada's 150th birthday, and looking back to 1967 and that old scrapbook will be interesting.

At the end of the school year, our teacher, Miss Van Westenbrugge, met with each of the grade 8 students individually in her office and gave us words of encouragement about the future. At that time, it was still my dream to become a teacher. Miss Van Westenbrugge was sure I would be a great teacher. Two year later, at her suggestion, I volunteered at the school, helping one of the teachers with an after-school art club. I enjoyed my interactions with the children and with the teacher. It was interesting being in the role of a leader in the classroom and observing the interactions among the staff members. I thought it gave me a clearer picture of what being a teacher might be like.

During my preteen and early teen years, I belonged to a girls' club at church. We were divided into groups, and each group had an older woman who was our counsellor. We did Bible study and crafts and worked on various projects to get badges for our scarves. As I've looked back on those years, I've realized the worth of the time the counsellors spent with us young girls. We became friends with our older sisters (our counsellors). One summer we all went camping together. We cooked on an outdoor fire, sang around the campfire and took long treks through the dunes to the beach. We all had fun, young and older. If in God's eyes one day is as a thousand years and a thousand years is as one day, it's no surprise that we can have great intergenerational fun times. It was good to learn that I could see older people as fellow travellers on our journey. And, as I get older, I can have friendships with younger people.

———

After spending all of my early years in Christian schools, I went to a public high school. Several of my former classmates were there, including Ellie, who had been a classmate in Wyoming. Girls had to wear skirts or dresses to school. Initially, I wore nylons with a garter belt, but as skirts were worn shorter and shorter, it became necessary to wear pantyhose. For gym class, we had to wear a "lovely" purple gym outfit.

I got along well with my peers, did quite well academically, and played the clarinet in the band for a few years. Math was one of my strong subjects, and I enjoyed learning languages, too. At the beginning of grade 12, I was taking English, French, German, Latin, and Greek. I found it too difficult to keep up the necessary vocabulary memorization for all those languages and wanted to drop Latin. My Latin teacher wanted me to continue. He even met with my parents and had me meet with the vice principal. However, I had made my decision and wouldn't change my mind. Looking back, I can see that at that point in my life, I knew what I wanted and wasn't afraid to state my case. I made acceptable choices even when others thought another way might be better.

I visited Mary a few times while she was at university, and I met her boyfriend, Ed. Mary planned to become a high school teacher and teach French and German. Later, during Mary's first year of teaching, I was in grade 12 and still thought I wanted to be a teacher. However, when I saw how much work Mary had to do outside of the classroom, I decided that teaching wasn't the career for me. I wanted a job that started when I got to work and ended when I went home.

Towards the end of grade 12, in 1971, our German teacher asked us if anyone was interested in having a pen pal in Germany. I was surprised to get a letter from Frank, who lived behind the Iron Curtain. The letters Frank and I sent could be monitored, so we had to be careful about what we wrote. It was an exciting time when Germany was unified and Frank began travelling to places that had earlier been unreachable to those behind the Iron Curtain. Frank is now married, with two sons and grandchildren. Our correspondence was more frequent initially, and there was a gap of a few years, but the connection remains. There have been a few phones calls, and gifts have been sent across the ocean, but we never had an opportunity to meet each other until—more much later.

———

When I was sixteen, one big challenge was trying to pass the driver's licence test. I passed on my third attempt. Dad and Mom sometimes allowed me to borrow their car for outings with my friends, not only to local places but also to events that were out of town. My parents felt it was important to have the freedom of being able to drive a car if you lived in the big country of Canada. Many years before, the day after she got her driver's licence, my mother had driven her four young children to visit a cousin an hour's drive away. I can still remember the adventure that day. I appreciated that my parents trusted in my abilities like my mother had once trusted in her own.

The summer of 1971 was a very busy time for me and my family. My parents celebrated their twenty-fifth wedding anniversary in June. The celebrations with my parents' friends and extended family were full of memories and laughter. Another celebration was on July 9, 1971, when Mary and Ed got married. I had been surprised and disbelieving initially when Mary asked me to be her maid of honour. When I realized she really meant the request, I was honoured. I began to realize that I was becoming a grown-up young lady!

During my high school years, I was more involved with youth group at church than in extracurricular activities at school. The summer of 1971, I went on Weekend Evangelism Team (WET) weekends with several other youth from nearby churches. I learned about the four spiritual laws, about getting deeper into God's Word, and about praying together for all things. It was an awesome time of sharing with others and evaluating my personal relationship with Jesus. One weekend, the team drove to Toronto to a Kathryn Kuhlman faith-healing service. Witnessing the power of the Holy Spirit at work during the service was a new experience for me.

One Sunday evening in August, my head knowledge about Jesus became heart knowledge, and He became Lord of my life. "For God so loved the world that he gave his one and only Son, that whoever believes in him shall not perish but have eternal life" (John 3:16). I had always known that Jesus loved me and that He was worthy of my trust, but now I could feel God's presence inside of me and I could worship Him in a whole new way. God's presence was abundant and sweet.

In early 1972, I decided to be part of a Summer Workshop in Ministries (SWIM) team. In the spring, I met Pastor Chris, who led the preparation workshop for our team of four girls. I didn't know it then, but Chris was a friend to the young man who would later become my husband. In the summer our SWIM team went to Grand Rapids, Michigan, to minister through the Eastern Avenue Christian Reformed Church. The church was in a ghetto area, and living and working there was a huge adjustment for all of us. We helped with Vacation Bible School in the mornings and did sessions of Backyard Story Time in the afternoons, a program we developed ourselves.

I was exposed to real-life situations I had never experienced before. We saw children who didn't cry when they fell, as no one cared. One evening, we were lying on the floor of our room as someone walked the street with a gun because he thought someone was messing with his wife. We witnessed how some people lived in that community so they could make a difference in the lives of others. We also learned that there has to be balance between work and play, especially when life is stressful. We spent time at Lake Michigan and went canoeing on some rivers in the northern peninsula of Michigan. Floating peacefully in a canoe down a quiet river was the perfect contrast to inner-city living.

SWIM was another life-changing experience for me. My life had always seemed quite secure and safe. It wasn't like that in the ghetto among unfamiliar people and troubling situations. I wasn't afraid, but my security couldn't come from my surroundings. It also couldn't come from my parents or other people. It had to come from within me, from my relationship with Father God. It was awesome to experience how, over the years, God moved me step by step into a deeper relationship with Him.

The enemy soon robbed me of some of my joy. While I was on SWIM, my father came to Grand Rapids for a meeting and brought my grade 13 report card. In those days, a student with an average of greater than 80 percent for all their marks was considered an Ontario scholar, which had a financial reward. I had been hoping my marks would be high enough. When I looked at my report card, all my marks were over 80—except for 79 in biology. It was obvious that I was an Ontario scholar. My father's remark was "Too bad that one mark wasn't over 80 too." Ouch! The root of rejection that had been planted so many years earlier began to sprout and grow. I began to struggle with feelings that I couldn't measure up to my parents' expectations of me.

Once I came home it was almost time to leave for my post-secondary education and after that start my career. It was another step in growing up and becoming an independent person. My jobs thus far had been doing housework for a family on Saturdays and babysitting during the summer months. I had also sometimes helped my father clean an office building on Friday evenings when he was working for a cleaning company. Now, for the first time, I felt concerned that maybe through my job choices I had disappointed my parents in some way.

The blessings of those years outweighed the challenges I faced in my later teens. As I look back on the Sarnia years of my life, I can see a blend of following parental guidance and making my own decisions. Much of what I learned from my parents was by example. Both Dad and Mom had a lot of life skills, were very organized, and seemed to enjoy the things they had to do, alone and together. They were involved in church activities and took time for family outings and for visiting with friends. If Dad and Mom had to work at their marriage, it certainly wasn't obvious to me, then or later. I wrongly assumed that my life would be like theirs when I grew up. God had different plans as He shaped and moulded me.

chapter four

A NURSING CAREER BEGINS

Trust in the LORD with all your heart and lean not on your own understanding; in all your ways submit to him, and he will make your paths straight.

—Proverbs 3:5–6

AFTER I REALIZED THAT I DIDN'T WANT TO BE A TEACHER, I HAD A DECISION to make. God must have been directing my steps when I chose a nursing career because I certainly didn't have much of an idea of what a nurse did. When my mother had surgery the summer before I started nursing school, I wasn't even a wee bit curious about her care or her caregivers. Although I had challenges while I was in nursing school, they weren't because I didn't enjoy the work I was doing.

In September of 1972, I started a two-year diploma nursing program in Chatham, Ontario. Before classes began, I had to order my student uniforms and all my textbooks. The price of textbooks has increased greatly over the years. For me, twelve text books cost a total of $106.71. The most expensive book was *The Textbook of Medical-Surgical Nursing* at $14.95. The uniforms and books were shipped to the school and were in my room at the nurses' residence when I arrived for the beginning of my classes.

My first challenge was my new living arrangements. I found it very difficult to be with my classmates all the time. Mary had left for university when I started high school, and I was used to a lot of quality "alone" time. In the residence, my room was close to a group of girls who weren't taking school very seriously, and the noise and silliness bothered me. I took advantage of any time when there was calm at my end of the hall. Therefore I wasn't watching TV with my classmates on Thursday, September 28, and I missed the hockey game when Paul Henderson scored the winning goal in the final game of the Canada-USSR hockey series. The sudden roar from the student lounge made me go investigate what had happened. I was sad that I missed that special Canadian moment.

My residence experience started to affect my classes. I told one of the instructors that I wasn't sure I would be able to stay at the school. I felt insecure about how I fit in and whether I could cope with where I lived. My parents connected with some people from the local Christian Reformed church and found me a place with room and board. I went to live with an older Dutch woman who also had other boarders. It was more like a family atmosphere. Many evenings we played board games for a while after supper. My room was a quiet space where I used my own desk from home. I could relax and even crocheted a teddy bear for my new niece. I once again had a safe haven to go to at the end of the day.

———

Right from the start, my favourite part of nursing was interacting with people. It felt good to see a smile on a face, to position someone more comfortably in their bed, or to help someone understand their situation just a wee bit better. I was very nervous about some of the skills I needed to learn, and it was a big challenge at times. My fingers are a bit double-jointed, and when I was nervous my fingers would lock at the most critical time. I conquered my fears enough to pass the skills aspect of the course and eventually became comfortable with the procedures I had to perform.

I remember one psychology class quite clearly. Our group of about twelve students was practising having a group session with the psychologist who was our instructor. When it was my turn to tell a bit about myself, I mentioned that my family was Dutch. The instructor interjected to explain to the group that since I was Dutch, I had been raised in a home with parents who were not affectionate and who didn't show their emotions. He added that I would have been affected by that. The father of lies once again whispered to me. He said, "You're not good enough, and there are good reasons why you're feeling so insecure right now!"

While the enemy was whispering lies to me, I was blessed to read two books by Walter Trobisch: *Love Yourself* and *Love Is a Feeling to Be Learned*. The short books are reflections on love and healthy self-acceptance and how it affects relationships and spiritual well-being. At the time, it was a peaceful feeling to let the words wash over me. There were still tough school days ahead, but the seeds of truth had been planted. In another season of my life I would need to once again focus on loving myself. I am a princess, a daughter of the great King!

While I was in nursing school, Dad found a job as a janitor at a Christian high school, which worked well for him. My parents and brothers moved to Hamilton, so my weekends at home were few. While I adjusted to my parents' move, school continued to be stressful. We started with a class of more than fifty students, and during the two years of my course, more than fifteen students were asked to leave. Two months before graduation, I once again felt like I wanted to leave school. With much encouragement from my parents, especially my father, I was able to complete my nursing course. Dad teasingly said that he deserved to be part RN. At the time, I didn't recognize my parents' support for the positive, wonderful gift it was.

During my two years in Chatham there were many weekend trips home. The bus ride from Sarnia to Chatham along the St. Clair River was a lovely trip on a dark evening, so many lights from the American side of the river reflecting off of the water. One evening, I wrote out songs and sayings of praise to God as I rode along the bumpy road. It made me smile when I recently found that sheet of paper among my archives. Most of my memories of nursing school had been of difficult, sad times. It was good to be reminded that I had been aware of the presence of God during those difficult days.

My best memories of nursing school are from the last weeks, when my friend Anita and I were assigned to work on a chronic floor. In those days, special care patients—who would now be in a long-term-care facility—were on a special unit in the hospital. Anita and I worked well together caring for the people assigned to our care. Two patients painted beautiful pictures, one with the brush in his mouth. Another patient, a quadriplegic, ran a stationery store from his room. It was positive activity in a difficult setting.

I enjoyed getting to know the staff and the personalities of the patients we cared for. At the end of our time there, Anita and I were a bit suspicious when many wheelchairs were lined up outside the shower room door. They threw us into the shower, which was a great way to end an otherwise stressful part of my life. My time on that unit made me more aware of the kind of nursing I wanted to do when I started my career.

———

On June 14, 1974, my classmates and I had our graduation with lots of pomp and ceremony. We all wore identical long-sleeved white uniforms and our caps with black bands. We each carried a bouquet of yellow roses with long purple ribbons. The ceremony was held in an old church that had a great atmosphere for the event. It was a proud and exciting evening. My parents, Mary and Ed, and four of my friends attended the ceremonies, and we continued the celebration afterwards. Several years later, I was told that nurses who graduated from the Chatham school "knew their stuff" and knew how to use common sense when making nursing decisions. God had definitely been guiding my steps.

chapter five

SINGLE ADULT YEARS

A person's steps are directed by the LORD. How then can anyone understand their own way?

—Proverbs 20:24

BEFORE MY GRADUATION, I ACCEPTED A JOB AT A HAMILTON HOSPITAL. DURING the interview I was asked what area I would like to work in. I responded that I wanted to work where I would be able to get to know patients and their families. I was offered and accepted a position on one of the neurosurgery units. My parents were still adjusting to life in Hamilton, and they invited me to live with them and my brothers. I hadn't planned to live at home again, but it seemed like a good idea while we all adjusted to a new place.

For the first few weeks of work, I either took the bus or borrowed Dad and Mom's car. Soon though, Dad and I went shopping at a used car lot near our home. My first car was a green automatic Toyota Corolla that I bought from a handsome salesman named Ralph Jones (some things you never forget!). The next spring I was able to buy a new car: a 1974 white Toyota Corolla. My new car had a four-speed manual transmission, which took a bit of getting used to. However, I dared to drive it to work the first day I had it. I even parked it on the third level of the parking garage, which was a bit of a challenge as there was lots of activity in the parking garage before my afternoon shift started.

The neurosurgical unit was a good place to start my career. Patients with spinal cord injuries or who had a craniotomy required lengthy hospital stays, and their families needed much support. My first head nurse gave me a piece of advice I've remembered often as I've needed to set priorities on a busy day. She said, "Make sure that everyone who should be alive is still alive when you go home."

I got very attached to some of the patients, especially the young ones with spinal cord injuries. I almost had a feeling of guilt for all the things I was able to do that those young people would never be able to do again. A friend told me that I was too consumed by my job. I realized that shift work was very absorbing of my time and energy, but I didn't recognize that I was too absorbed emotionally as well.

At the end of my first year of nursing, I wanted to gain more and different experiences. I no longer remember why I wanted a big adventure at the age of twenty-one. Perhaps God knew that because of my deep attachment to some spinal cord patients, a big change was necessary. I applied for and got a job at a nine-bed hospital in Kyle, Saskatchewan, which had a population of five hundred.

My brother Clarence shared the driving when I went to Kyle, but first we drove east to visit Margie (Huizinga) and Stuart VanderVaart in Deep River, Ontario. At their wedding, in May of 1975, I had been Margie's maid of honour. Our friendship had started many years before when our families visited each other and had grown in more significant ways during our youth group years. While in Deep River, I sat beside the Ottawa River while everyone else went canoeing because I couldn't stop thinking about the quadriplegic patients I had cared for. After recognizing how unhealthy my feelings were, I learned to detach myself from my patients more effectively.

As Clarence and I travelled west to Kyle, it was interesting to experience the sudden change in the landscape. We transitioned from the lakes and trees of northern Ontario to Canada's prairie land. Clarence and I took turns driving and reading the book *Sybil* by Flora Rheta Schreiber. Sometimes the driver got impatient for his or her next turn to read. After spending a day or two in Kyle, Clarence flew back to Ontario out of Saskatoon, a two-hour drive from Kyle but the nearest major city.

When I had applied for the position, Kyle-White Bear Union Hospital was an active hospital with lots of opportunities for learning. However, there was a change in doctors before I arrived. The new doctor (from another country) had few privileges, so there was very little activity. On evening and night shifts, there was only one nurse working. I normally enjoyed alone time, but I had too much of a good thing while living in Kyle. I was glad that it was harvest time and there was lots of activity on the fields. However, I had difficulty adjusting to the isolation—small town, small hospital, vast open spaces where everything was far apart. Sometimes there were only one or two patients in the hospital. Luckily, when a woman came in to deliver her baby, the baby arrived before the nurse from the previous shift went home.

When I knew I needed a change, I applied for jobs in the cities of Regina and Saskatoon, but they weren't hiring nurses. So, after one month, knowing that driving back to Ontario in the winter wouldn't be an option, I made the decision to return at the end of October. I have no regrets about the experience. I visited the cities of Regina and Saskatoon, saw awesome sunrises and sunsets, visited a Hutterite colony, and spent many hours walking in the coulees of the South Saskatchewan River.

For my return to Ontario, my father flew out to Regina to help me drive my car back to Ontario. I worked for four hours on a Friday morning and then went to Regina to pick Dad up from the airport at 3:00 p.m. Then we drove and drove and drove for thirty-two hours. We sang and talked as we took turns driving: a father's love in action. On Saturday evening, when we were quite close to home, Dad said he was too tired to drive anymore. I said I could keep driving if he could stay awake to keep talking to me. We arrived home at about eleven that night, two days after Mom's birthday. Family at home had just decided that if Dad and I were daring enough to drive without stopping, we would arrive soon—and there we were. From Kyle, Saskatchewan, to Winnipeg, Manitoba, to Thunder Bay, Ontario, to Hamilton, Ontario, is 3,024 kilometres.

———

The Hamilton hospital I had left a few months earlier rehired me, and I was welcome to live with my parents again. I now worked in the burn unit. This was most definitely a place where I got to know patients and their families. It was an intense place to work, with critically ill patients and often members of the same family being cared for at the same time.

Few nurses worked there for an extended period of time. One young man was very badly burned after wrapping a blanket around his cousin, whose clothes were burning. There was nothing available for him when his clothes caught on fire too. One night, as he was dying at the age of seventeen, he talked about his faith. Then he said to me, "It's okay, Annette, because I'm ready to die and my cousin isn't." I hope that sharing that with me blessed him as much as it did me. He expressed no anger, no regrets; he just showed peace. It's a story I have shared often over the years.

Nursing continued to be an all-consuming career for me, but in a healthier way than previously. I was both emotionally and physically exhausted at the end of a shift. I don't think my parents realized this. They seemed concerned that I wasn't getting involved with more activities outside of work. The situation was compounded by how difficult it was to find things to get involved in when I was working shifts and weekends. I'm sure that they only wanted what they thought was best for me, but it made me feel like I was disappointing them. I was trying, but I felt like it wasn't enough, for them or for me. As a teenager, I had noticed that Dad would rub his fused wrist when he was stressed. I didn't want to be the cause of him having more pain, so I never talked to my parents about how I was feeling. Unfortunately, I carried the practice of not discussing my feelings into other relationships in my life, too.

I was able to enjoy some activities. I had learned to sew during my mid-teens, and I bought my own sewing machine and sewed most of my clothes: pants, blouses, dresses and light jackets. Dad and Mom hadn't taken their piano to Hamilton, and I missed it, so I bought myself a piano. I did lots of reading, took a night school course at local community college one semester and also sang in the same choir that Dad did for a while.

In the fall of 1977, I went on a three-week trip to the Netherlands. Relatives on both sides of the family made sure I met as many of them as possible. It was great to feel a deep connection to my far-away family and to have another opportunity to see Opa, Dad's father. I was shown family burial places and homes my parents had lived in. I became more aware of

God's faithfulness through the generations. I also saw many local attractions. There were forests, farms, peat bogs and fields with heather; there were windmills, canals, ducks on water and warm, friendly people.

Some of my vacation experiences had lasting benefits. During that trip I learned how to communicate much better in the Dutch language, and I've been able to translate for Dutch-speaking patients when needed. Two of Dad's brothers and their wives gave me a pattern for a cross-stitch letter "A" when I visited their hobby store. It was the beginning of my love for cross-stitching. When I got married, Dad's siblings gave me a tablecloth I could cross-stitch.

These were searching years of trying to discover what God wanted for my life. It was probably in 1976 that I noticed an opening with Christian Reformed World Relief Committee (now World Renew) for a health teaching position in Haiti. I went to Grand Rapids, Michigan, twice. First I was interviewed for the position, and later I met with the nurse who was already working in Haiti. The process took many, many months. After much thought and prayer, I decided that going to Haiti wasn't right for me. What I really wanted was to be a wife and mother, to have a life-partner like Dad and Mom had. Going to Haiti wasn't part of that dream. I realize now that I probably wasn't ready for Haiti in other ways as well. Being a leader on the mission field would probably have been too big a challenge for me to handle at that time.

Except for the brief time in Saskatchewan, I lived at my parents' home for the first four years after I started working. I would soon be the only child still living at home. By the spring of 1978, Len was at school in Michigan, where he planned to attend Calvin Seminary, and Clarence was getting married to Jeri. I felt that it was time for me to spread my wings once again, hopefully more permanently this time.

Dad felt strongly about me not living in the same city they lived in if I no longer wished to live at home, so it was necessary for me to look for another job as well. I was burnt-out from working on the burn unit, so moving on was probably a good thing anyway. I decided to move back to Sarnia so my surroundings would be familiar. Sarnia was also closer to Mary and her family in Strathroy. Mary had two little ones at home and was expecting twins in the fall, and I would be more easily able to help her. I was hired for a position at Sarnia General Hospital, where I had been born in. Soon I bought some furniture and found a one-bedroom apartment. I moved after being a bridesmaid at Clarence and Jeri's wedding.

It was fun decorating my own place and learning to cook for one person. My friends from my younger years no longer lived in Sarnia, but I got involved in of some of the activities I had enjoyed. I had great memories of camping with my parents. One time when we camped near Collingwood it was so windy that my father said it was like sleeping inside an accordion. I appreciate that they borrowed camping equipment and made the effort. Sarnia was close to Lakewood Christian Campground where I had gone camping with my youth group in the past. That summer, I bought some equipment and went camping with my friend Margo and with Mary's children. For me, camping was a time of quiet and restoration, especially around a campfire or viewing the immensity of a starry sky.

In the fall, it was a beautiful drive from Sarnia to Strathroy. The new highway went through land that had once been the woods at the back of our farm. The yellows, reds and oranges of the fall leaves were awesome. I tried to visit more often over the weeks and months after Mary's twin boys were born. One day, my oldest nephew said to me, "Auntie Nette, I think two babies are too many. I think they should bring one back." I invited him to my apartment for an overnight visit ,and he had some one-on-one attention, even from the firemen at the fire station. My niece, his older sister, had her turn, too. I was glad that I had bought a pull-out sofa.

At the hospital, I worked on any unit, on any day I was needed. When I worked in the surgical day care unit, I was told that those rooms had been the delivery rooms in the past. It was strange to think that I was giving nursing care in one of the rooms I had been born in. My father had been in a waiting room somewhere nearby, anxiously waiting for news of my arrival. It was even longer before he had a chance to hold me.

He was only allowed to look at me in the nursery until my mother and I went home.

At the hospital, I took a critical care course on my own time, often missing opportunities to work shifts that I would have been paid for. Participants were promised a full-time job at the end of our classes as a new cardiac care unit was opening. However, at the end of the course, I was offered a work schedule that was thirteen shifts in three weeks, two shifts short of full-time. I would not be entitled to benefits, paid vacations or paid sick time. It was upsetting news. I resigned. I would use that critical care knowledge elsewhere at another time.

I was still searching. I decided to move on again, this time to a larger city. I had felt lonelier and more isolated in Sarnia than I had anticipated. Soon my piano and other furniture were being moved once again. I'm humbled when I think of how often my family helped me move without complaining. I found a full-time job in St. Joseph's Hospital in London, Ontario. I was still close enough to Mary and her family for frequent visits and closer to my parents' home in Hamilton.

I started my new job after my brother Len and Nienke got married. I worked full-time on a forty-four-bed urology unit. It was very busy but a fun place to work, even though I didn't get to know many patients or their families. Patients came in for surgery, were in hospital for a few days, and went home. Many years later, some of the skills and knowledge I had gained were useful when working with renal patients and when doing home health care. It was great to be reminded that with God nothing is wasted.

Many of the nurses on my unit at St. Joe's were single, mid-twenties, like I was. We went out for pizza a few times after working evenings and to the Shakespearean Theatre in Stratford to see a play. I joined a young adults group at church. I was within walking distance of downtown and a short drive from Springbank Park, and I enjoyed getting some exercise on days off. Moving to London brought my life some of the benefits I had hoped for.

When my friend Margo visited from Hamilton, we decided to go for an overnight trip to Detroit, Michigan. We toured the Henry Ford Museum and Greenfield Village. We had a great time.

On our way home we headed east instead of west and didn't notice for a long time, about one and a half hours. First we almost ran out of gas, and then we noticed we had very little US money to buy gas. It was getting late in the day, and Margo had to work in Hamilton the next day.

For some reason this all seemed very funny. We were almost giddy with silliness by the time we crossed the border at Sarnia and passed near Ed and Mary's home in Strathroy. We were sure they would want to know about our adventures, so we drove to their home and threw stones at their bedroom window to get their attention. After more giddy laughter we finally returned to London, and Margo left for Hamilton. Margo has since married and moved to Thunder Bay, but this is one adventure that we haven't forgotten—and neither have Ed and Mary.

I had dated very seldom during my teens but didn't miss it because I had great times with my youth group friends. After I started working, all my energy was absorbed by my career initially, and when I had more energy, I found it difficult to get involved because of working shifts and weekends. Therefore, when I saw a personal ad in a church-related magazine in September of 1979, I responded to it. A professional man, age thirty-two, was looking for an "understanding" woman to connect with.

My letter had to be mailed to a box number assigned by the magazine and forwarded to the man, and then that man had to mail a response to me. When a response finally came, it was from Bob in Alberta, who did specialized repairs in a hospital. He was six and a half years older than me and, like me, was Dutch and attended a Christian Reformed Church. He had lived in Ontario most of his life. Bob didn't mention his mother in our communications, and I didn't realize that she was still alive for the first six months we were connecting. It was when Bob was planning a trip to Ontario to visit friends and family that I became aware that his mother didn't live far from where I lived.

Later, I learned that Bob was born in the Netherlands. Because of the death of his father when he was nine months old, he had lived with his maternal grandmother and his mother's unmarried brother and sister during his early years. His life changed greatly when he was six years old when his mother emigrated to Canada with him and his older sister. In Canada, Bob's mother married a bachelor, and they added four adopted children to the family.

We wrote many letters, which were soon passing each other. It was sometimes a bit confusing. Very early on, there was a letter that made me wonder if I should have concerns about having a relationship with Bob. I wondered if he had problems feeling loved and accepted. Those feelings were soon gone in all our exploring of thoughts and ideas, which later included long conversations on the phone too. Bob was unhappy about several things in his life, but he seemed hopeful that things would get better in the right circumstances.

Bob decided to come to Ontario for the month of April 1980. He planned to spend time with his eldest sister's family and his friend Chris, whom I had met through my SWIM experience. Pastor Chris now lived in Florida. Bob planned to drive from Alberta to Ontario and then to Florida. We would decide how much time we wanted to spend together after we met. I had some vacation days during that time, so we had some options. It was a scary and exciting time as I anticipated his arrival. I didn't really know Bob yet, but the relationship had become very important to me.

Bob arrived at my apartment on a Monday afternoon, carrying a framed photo he had taken of a cactus flower. There was some love poetry by Kahlil Gibran taped to the back of the photo, and he also had a little bag of marshmallows. He had brought me flowers, poetry and candy! I was impressed! We went for a walk, had supper, and decided he would return on the weekend when I had days off again.

During Bob's four weeks of vacation, he visited some family and friends on his own, and we visited many people together. By the end of the month, Bob had met my family and I had met his. We also did some sightseeing and had an enjoyable time in everything we did. My family and friends liked Bob, and he seemed to get along well with all of them.

His mother and sister seemed to have reservations about our relationship, but I didn't put too much significance on that. At the end of the month, Bob proposed marriage to me, and I accepted. The next morning Bob left to drive back to Alberta.

We saw each other again a few weeks later when I flew to Alberta for the May long weekend. We toured some of the city where Bob lived, which I thought would someday be my home, and went camping in the Rocky Mountains near Banff. I'm sure the views were glorious, but I felt closed in by the mountains. I felt even more closed in later that weekend when Mount St. Helens, in Washington State, erupted and the skies became darker. I was glad I wouldn't be living too close to those mountains.

Bob and I had a good time together that weekend. He was knowledgeable about the places we visited and shared a lot of information. There was one rough patch, though, when I wondered if I was looking at my future properly. I didn't seem to be able to talk to Bob about that, and those feelings were set aside. We did talk about when we would get married. Bob wanted to get married in June; yikes, that seemed way too soon to me! We settled on September 12, 1980, less than seventeen weeks away. There were many plans and many decisions to be made in the following weeks and months.

In hindsight, I can see that "loving each other dearly" did not describe my relationship with Bob at that point. I was trusting that the bond between us would grow deeper and stronger in the years ahead.

———

A former colleague offered Bob a maintenance job in Kingston, Ontario, which he accepted. He hoped to get back into specialized repairs in the future. He was glad to return to Ontario, and I was glad I didn't have to move to Alberta. In July, after selling most of his furniture in Alberta, Bob drove to Ontario, pulling a tent trailer behind his little car. He had extra items tied wherever he could so he could move as many things as possible. I imagine it was a bit scary for anyone following him on the highway. Before our wedding we were able to find a short-lease apartment near Kingston. We hoped to buy our first home soon.

chapter six
MARRIED—THE KINGSTON YEARS

The light shines in the darkness, and the darkness has not overcome it.
—John 1:5

BOB AND I WERE MARRIED IN HAMILTON, IN MY PARENTS' CHURCH, ON September 12, 1980. Bob was very pleased that Pastor Chris was able to come from Florida to officiate at our wedding. Chris had been Bob's supporter, friend, and surrogate father for many years. Mary was my matron of honour, and John, a lifelong friend of Bob's, was best man. Our guest list was short, as we didn't have many mutual friends and we liked the idea of a small wedding. We planned a Friday evening service, with a reception and late lunch to follow.

Our wedding service included hymns, a duet by Clarence and Jeri, and a message by Pastor Chris. Chris's message was based on "The light shines in the darkness, and the darkness has not overcome it" (John 1:5). This was not the Bible verse that Bob and I had chosen for Chris to use, but there must have been a reason for the change. For many years that verse was a blessing for me. It helped me trust that the light would overcome when life felt dark.

There was a huge surprise at our wedding. Two of Bob's uncles and a cousin came from the Netherlands. Bob had tears in his eyes when I came down the aisle, not because of the sight of me—sigh—but because he was so touched by his uncles being there. My family had known about the arrivals the day before and rearranged some of the seating at the reception to accommodate our Dutch-speaking guests. It was an enjoyable evening for all who attended.

Bob made reservations at a nearby hotel for the first two nights of our marriage. It was there that I lost my virginity, and I'm thankful that Bob respected my wishes in that area. There had been times of great temptation, but together we were able to make waiting possible. We also gave each other wedding gifts that evening. I had spent many hours sewing Bob a new housecoat. It wasn't fancy, but I thought he might consider it a useful personal gift. Bob gave me a pressure cooker. I hadn't expected something quite that impersonal! In later years, I was able to laugh about the appropriateness of it, God's surprising humour about a difficult situation. (A secondary meaning of "pressure cooker" is a situation or atmosphere of difficulty, stress, or anxiety.)

On the second evening of our marriage, Bob and I went out for dinner at a steak house. The atmosphere was nice and cozy, and I was feeling friendly and comfortable. Our waiter was a pleasant young man who was easy to engage in chitchat as he took our order and brought us our food. When we got back to our hotel room, Bob told me that I had been much too friendly with the waiter. He said I didn't know how to behave in the situation and we would never be able to go to a nice restaurant again. I was shocked and hurt. I thought what he said wasn't true, but I didn't know what to do or say. For a long time, I was too embarrassed to tell anyone else what had happened.

Something broke inside of me that night. I had imagined that our relationship would grow deeper and stronger as we learned to know each other better and trust each other more. My parents had an awesome relationship, and they had made marriage seem easy, but they hadn't shown me how to handle disagreements or conflict in a marriage. I became focused on protecting myself from further hurt and rejection. The same girl who had not talked to her parents about her feelings was burying her feelings again.

The next day, the first Sunday of our married life, was spent with family and friends who had come for our wedding. I gave no hint of the turmoil inside of me. Bob and I heard my brother Len preach in Dad and Mom's church in the morning service; in the evening we heard Chris preach in the church he and Bob had attended years earlier. Bob and I had not made detailed plans for our honeymoon, so we were able to include some time visiting with Bob's Dutch uncles. I had looked forward to our time away after the busyness of preparing for our wedding, but I was never able to fully relax. I was on the alert for the next put-down.

———

Soon we were settling in eastern Ontario. Bob was working every day and taking night school courses at the local community college. I got a casual position at Kingston General Hospital. Because I was willing to work on any unit, I was able to pick when I wanted to work and only had to work one weekend a month. There was a lot of variety, which I enjoyed. However, I had no opportunity to get connected with any staff members.

We attended the Kingston Christian Reformed Church when we were at home, but we often went away on weekends, visiting family and friends. It was a disjointed, busy schedule, which did little to help us grow as a couple or to help me develop any friendships. Bob and I were also not finding a common ground in our faith walk, even though we had grown up in the same denomination. I viewed Bob as being legalistic and lacking in joy; he viewed me as being too accepting of sin in the lives of others. Life was different than I had dreamed or expected it to be.

———

In December, Bob and I moved into our first home. We bought a one-and-a-half-storey three-bedroom house. We had a long, narrow yard with lots of perennials and a small vegetable garden. I enjoyed caring for the vegetable garden and pulling lots of plants and weeds out of the perennial beds to reclaim them from chaos. It was home, a good space to share with family and friends when there was opportunity. Kingston was a long drive from most of those nearest and dearest to us but much better than Alberta would have been.

In March of 1981, six months after we were married, Bob wanted to attend a marriage enrichment weekend. We had just found out that I was pregnant, and I had many conflicting emotions. I was excited about having a baby but sad that Bob was unhappy with our marriage. I was trying my best. My biggest problem, though, was that I was embarrassed to go to an enrichment weekend so soon after our wedding. I felt better when I found out that another young couple at the retreat had been married more recently than we had. (Now I think that any time is a good time to enrich your marriage!)

It was an enjoyable weekend, and Bob and I gained some new insights into each other. When we were asked to draw a picture of our home, Bob drew the inside of the house and I drew the outside. I no longer remember the significance of that, but it was the first of an often repeated situation. Bob and I gained some new insights and felt better about our life together for a while. However, our new insights didn't lead to changes in how we related to each other, so the problems weren't resolved.

During my pregnancy I had two ultrasounds because my doctor was convinced at one point that I was having twins. My family has a strong history of twins—my paternal grandparents had two sets of twin sons, my father was a twin, my brothers were twins, and my mother and sister had both given birth to twins. On one of my last prenatal visits, Dr. Swift said that he would be sure there was only one baby if I delivered one baby and there were "no more babies in there." So I bought some extra diapers. My due date was October 13, but I didn't go into labour until October 22, late in the afternoon.

Bob was with me when I was admitted to the hospital at 7:00 p.m. By 9:00 p.m. I sensed that something was wrong. I had some obstetrics knowledge from nurses' training, and what I was experiencing didn't seem to fit with what I had read or seen. When Bob went to get a nurse, the team was involved with an emergency with another mother. Later, when help arrived, they "broke my water" and realized that our baby was in distress. Soon they moved me to another room for closer monitoring. By three the next morning, blood had been taken from our baby's scalp veins. When the results came back, I was immediately rushed into the operating room for an emergency Caesarean section (C-section). The level of oxygen in our baby's blood had been much too low.

Welcome, Ian!

Ian Christian, named after Bob's father and Pastor Chris, was born at 3:19 a.m. on October 23, 1981, weighing seven pounds and nine ounces. Bob hadn't been allowed in the operating room, but he did get to see Ian as he was whisked away to the Neonatal Intensive Care Unit (NICU). When I awoke from the anaesthetic, I was told that they had resuscitated Ian for nine minutes before he started breathing on his own. Dr. Swift had been there praying throughout. Later, Dr. Swift explained to me that the umbilical cord had been tightly wrapped around Ian's neck. This explained why my labour had been different. My body had been trying to push the baby out, but the cord was pulling him back.

I was awed by my first glimpse of our precious son. He was tiny, with very blue eyes and fuzzy strawberry blond hair. (He later was very blond.) Another thing I noticed was that he was so "there," so bright and alert. It was a huge blessing after the scare I had so recently been told about. He continued to be monitored by the NICU staff during our hospital stay, but he spent many hours with me. Initially, moving about was a bit of a challenge because of my surgery, but soon I was a little more mobile and able to take over Ian's care.

Dad and Mom arrived the morning after Ian's arrival to meet their newest grandson. Dad was thrilled when he was allowed to hold Ian. This was the youngest baby he had held since my sister was born, more than thirty-two years earlier. Dad loved babies! It was a precious moment, and I can still picture Dad in a yellow gown, holding his newest grandson. It was great to share that special time with my parents.

Four or five days after Ian's birth, I was having a difficult time. The problem was probably a bit hormonal, a bit about the shock of the circumstances of Ian's birth, and a bit because of my lengthy hospital stay after a C-section. However, it was mostly because I was very concerned about Bob. He seemed to be feeling *very* down about life. I talked to Dr. Swift about my concerns, and he asked to see Bob in his office before I was discharged from the hospital. Apparently, at that appointment, Bob said that his main stressor was the state of our marriage. A marriage counselling appointment was set up for shortly after my discharge.

It was a difficult homecoming for me: a newborn baby to care for after a C-section, a house that hadn't been cared for in a week, and a husband who wasn't happy about his life. Ian was an awesome baby and brought much joy to my life, but he was sometimes affected by the stress I was feeling. I felt like I was failing not only as a wife but as a mother too.

Our first marriage counselling sessions were through the Family Medicine program at Queen's University. Bob and I saw two different family practice residents, one before Christmas and one after. The first doctor we saw suggested to me, in a private session, that I get out of the marriage right away as he saw no future in it. I certainly wasn't ready to make that decision. I had a newborn baby, and the counsellor wasn't a Christian, so I had good reasons for ignoring his advice. The second doctor did some assertiveness training with us. This helped us recognize a problem, but again there was no work towards a solution. We were able to move forward with some semblance of hope, though.

Life settled into a routine of work and night school for Bob and caring for an infant and a home for me. When Ian was seven months old, I returned to work on a casual basis at Kingston General Hospital. Bob enjoyed the times he had to care for Ian. During the week, I shared babysitting duties with Beth, another nurse, who also had a young son. We planned our schedules so we worked opposite days.

Another change was that we started attending the Kingston Christian Fellowship, a small charismatic group of about twenty families. We were made very welcome, and it was a blessing to us at that time. At first the worship with so much emphasis on the Holy Spirit was a bit overwhelming, but soon I was being richly blessed. During our time at the Fellowship, I received my own prayer language. There were many times when I didn't know what I needed or wanted from God, and it was a comfort to know that He was hearing the cries of my heart that I couldn't articulate.

Bob and I sometimes had the young adults group from the Fellowship over for lunch on Sundays. It was good to feel connected to these people and to share the food I had prepared with others. I enjoyed cooking, baking, canning and freezing fruit and vegetables and making pickles and jams. All these activities added to my busyness, but they helped make our house a home. They were part of my dream of being a wife and mother. It was good to have these times of feeling positive about what I was accomplishing.

———

Shortly after we bought our home, we had urea-formaldehyde foam insulation (UFFI) put into our home. This soon became a huge problem as UFFI was banned because of health concerns. Bob was very unhappy with his job and wanted to look for work in specialized repairs again, but we were unable to sell our home if a move was necessary. We were blessed when grants became available for removing the foam. With the money we were promised we would be able to cover much of the cost of removing the wood siding and UFFI from our home and replace it with new insulation and vinyl siding. Before our grant money even arrived, Bob started a job in his field of choice at a Kingston hospital. I hoped that Bob would feel much better about his life with his new job.

———

When I suspected I might be pregnant again, I took a urine sample to the doctor's office. When I called for the results, I was told that Dr. Swift wanted to talk to me himself and he would call me later. When he called, he said, "Annette, I hate to tell you this, but you are pregnant again." My immediate response was to deny that this was a problem for me. I told Dr. Swift that I realized my life had challenges. However, for me, the situation made it more important than ever for Ian to have a sibling. I didn't know where the road of life would take us, but I didn't think it would be ideal for Ian to be an only child. I didn't allow my mind to process that thought further.

Welcome, Leona!

This baby took extra time to arrive as well. Dr. Swift called me a "slow cooker." My due date was April 23, but it was many days before I was admitted to the hospital. Ian stayed with Beth, the babysitter, when I went into the hospital. I had a trial of labour, which was unsuccessful, and then another C-section. This time I had an epidural anaesthetic, and I was aware of our baby's birth. Our daughter, Leona Jentina, named after my parents, was delivered at 6:19 p.m. on May 10, 1983, weighing eight pounds and one ounce. I hadn't been aware how much I hoped for a little girl. God had granted the desire of my heart and surprised me with joy. She was a blue-eyed wonder with very fine blonde hair. Like her brother, she was very "there" right from the start. Soon Dad and Mom came to meet their new granddaughter.

Bob's new job hadn't helped make the changes I had prayed for. While I was still in the hospital, Bob told me that he found it easier at home without me there. It was a difficult thing to hear. Near the end of my hospital stay, Ian was ill with a fever, which Dr. Swift felt was an emotional response from missing me. I needed to go home; that was where I belonged.

Physically, I was stronger than I had been after my first C-section, and I was very happy about that. Emotionally, I was overwhelmed and lonely. On the morning of Leona's and my discharge, Bob and Ian came to the hospital early so Bob could go to work for the rest of the day. Oma, Bob's mother, had planned to come to help me for a few days, but she had fallen and broken a hip.

It was a sad morning after we arrived at home. Ian was still not feeling well. I wasn't allowed to pick him up after my C-section because he was too heavy. We sat on the floor, held each other, and cried. I'm quite sure the emotional release was good for both of us. Life improved greatly six days later when my mother came to stay for a few days.

Ian was eighteen and a half months old when Leona was born, so there were many busy days and nights. Bob would play with Ian for a while when he got home from work but continued to take night school courses. Most evenings, he was either gone or he had homework to do. The lawn seemed especially large that year—so little time and sometimes so little energy. Leona was fussy on hot days. I moved her inside, outside, put her in the buggy, in her crib, in her sitter. It was challenging. I added to the stress by keeping inside all my frustration that I wasn't getting more help from Bob with yard work and childcare.

At the beginning of August, we took our tent trailer out for our first family camping expedition. Bob always felt a need to get out and do things, and this was something we could do as a family. I enjoyed the distraction of getting organized for the adventure. The children tolerated the experience extremely well, and getting away from home for a weekend was good. It was the first of many camping outings.

Bob had vacation time later in August and told me that he needed to go to Alberta to visit old friends. He would do this with or without his family; it was up to me. It was a difficult decision to make. Ian was twenty-two months old and Leona was three months old. Even though we had had a successful camping trip, I knew it would be very challenging to drive from Ontario to Alberta with two very small children. I also knew it would be difficult to be at home by myself with two wee ones for three or four weeks. In the end, I was more comfortable with people thinking I was courageous or stupid than I was with what people would think if Bob went to Alberta alone. Preparing for the trip west added to the busyness of my already busy summer, and there was more to come.

Before we left for our trip to Alberta, too many things were happening. The renovation started for the removal of the UFFI from our home. At the time of our departure to Alberta, the wood siding and UFFI had been removed, but new insulation and vinyl siding still needed to be installed. Oma arrived a few days before we left. She was recuperating from her hip pinning and still had major mobility issues. She needed help with bathing and other things. Bob's middle sister, who lived in Kingston, would take over Oma's care in our home while we were gone.

There were many things for me to do. I had to prepare for people staying in our home and for my family's trip to Alberta, all in a house under renovation. The final challenge was when Bob's sister decided we should have friends over for supper the evening before we left for Alberta. When I look back, I know it was God who gave me strength to do the things I had to do. Even He must have wondered if I had forgotten how to say no!

On the drive to Alberta, we stopped to see friends along the way. We had a nice visit with Margo and her family in Thunder Bay and also stopped in Saskatoon to see Bob's friend Dee and her family. When we arrived in Alberta, there were several other people Bob wanted to connect with, but it was awkward with a young family in tow. Our trip did not go well.

At one point, Bob left the kids and me in a motel room. I didn't feel confident he was coming back, and I tried to figure out how the kids and I would get back to Ontario without him. He came back very excited because he had seen some of his "guy friends." I couldn't make myself share in his pleasure. I was blamed for trying to interfere with his relationships with his friends. I'm sure that being very tired was part of my problem, but it was a very lonely, scary time.

On our drive home things settled back into "normal." Ian and Leona tolerated the long drive quite well, and I continued on, putting one foot in front of each other and living each day as it came.

After our return, Bob was working and attending night school classes, but he was deeply unhappy. The trip west hadn't given him the emotional boost that he had hoped it would. He planned to take a leave of absence from work and go to Florida to visit our friend Pastor Chris. Ian and Leona had a respiratory illness at the time, and I didn't like the idea of being left at home with two wee ones. I asked for prayer at a prayer meeting at our church, the Fellowship. The men tried to remind Bob of his responsibilities as the head of family. Bob resented their interference. His need for "a boost" was too great for him to stay home.

While Bob was in Florida, Chris told him that he shouldn't have left me at home. Bob again told me he resented my interference with his friendships. While he was gone, I had difficult days caring for two sick young children, struggling to give them the antibiotics they needed and dealing with feelings of desertion and lack of support. In the midst of it all, I was reminded that God loves me more than I could ever imagine. One evening, I attended a Bible study with friends from the Fellowship. We talked about the impact that things happening at home were having on my life. They had a special prayer time for me and prayed that God would be my glory and the lifter of my head (Psalm 3:3). I felt my head go up physically as they were praying. I was reminded that I could walk proud as a daughter of the Great King. I was not a failure. I was dearly loved and never alone.

———

During the early years of Ian's and Leona's lives, I enjoyed watching them grow and change. Ian always enjoyed his little sister, but life was more fun after they could do more together. There were lots of toy messes to clear up at the end of each day, but it was worth it. Inside or outside, they knew how to have fun together.

During quiet days at home, I was able to indulge my creative side. I made a crib quilt for each of my children and sewed some clothes for them. It was fun making matching outfits, one with ruffles and one without. However, I often found myself becoming anxious when it was time for Bob to come home from work. Which Bob would be coming home? Would it be the one who was present with us or the one who ignored us? Would he again threaten to quit his job?

I had grown up with parents who lived and worked well together. I kept trying harder myself, but I had no idea how to work *with* Bob to make things better. There was always a lot of internal confusion for me as I tried to be loyal to Bob but also realized that I was not comfortable with his reactions to life situations and his behaviour.

Bob was often unhappy and depressed, and I did more of the decorating, yard work and snow shovelling than I ever imagined I would have to. I didn't mind doing those tasks; in fact, I enjoyed doing them. However, with small children at home, I didn't have enough energy to do all the outdoor and indoor work. I also didn't feel appreciated and therefore felt little joy in the things I accomplished.

At times when Bob felt very badly, he would binge drink. If he drank at home, he would listen to the same Marty Robbins album over and over. I lay in bed and cringed when I heard the music start. The worst, however, was when he went out to drink. I was very upset and concerned because he was driving home drunk. There was no sleep for me until he returned home and was safe in bed.

Bob no longer felt welcome at the Fellowship, so he joined a Bible study and started attending another church. Now that he was gone for Bible study as well as night school, he was seldom home in the evenings unless he was doing homework for school or sleeping. Communication between us was almost non-existent. It didn't feel like the children and I were really a part of his life, except to make him feel a little less alone at times. For a while he attended one church and Ian and Leona went to the Fellowship with me. It seemed to be what worked best for our family at the time.

Around the same time that Bob started attending the Bible study, I started working in the operating room at Kingston Penitentiary every Wednesday from 8 a.m. to 4 p.m. One of the women at the Fellowship was employed there, and I heard about the position through her. The job wasn't especially challenging, as only simple surgeries were done there, but it was a huge blessing for me. I felt respected and appreciated in the workplace. It was good to be in a totally different environment for a day each week, away from the stressors at home.

One day I was whistling as I worked. An inmate kindly but firmly said to me, "I'll warn you that you don't whistle in here." I didn't ask questions, and I didn't whistle again. I wasn't afraid of working in the prison environment though. I had previously worked in a downtown Hamilton hospital where I had cared for out-of-control alcoholics and members of motorcycle gangs. It was especially tense when members of two opposing gangs were on the unit at the same time. In the penitentiary, although the stories of the men I cared for were sometimes horrific, it felt safer because a guard was present.

There was one exception to that. An inmate who had recently attacked a guard came for treatment. He was attended by three guards while he awaited surgery. After the inmate had anaesthetic, two guards left, as they couldn't justify staying during the operation. I was assigned to stay with the inmate after his surgery, as he was the last case of the day. While the one remaining guard left to get the others, the inmate regained consciousness. He looked at me and asked, "Is it just you and me here?"

Very calmly, I said, "Yes, but I'm sure the others will be here very shortly."

The guards apologized profusely when they returned.

I also had opportunities to see other areas of the prison. After a hostage-taking, I worked two weekend shifts and delivered medications to inmates in their cells and those in solitary confinement. One afternoon I went with another nurse to check all the first aid boxes and saw all the inmate workshops. I thank God for finding such a unique place for me to spend time during this difficult season. It was the most interesting job of my nursing career.

Another blessing was visits from our friends and family. During the summer months we often had guests who were sightseeing in the Kingston area. People would stay for a few days or just drop by. Several times there were guests from the Netherlands. Menu planning and meal preparation were rewarding, and it was fun to sit around the dining room table at suppertime and hear about the adventures of their day. Going for a Thousand Island tour was especially popular, and our family accompanied our guests several times. It was a great way to spend a peaceful Saturday afternoon.

It seemed we always had to be busy: visiting, going places, doing things. I think it made us feel like we were "normal" if we had stories to share. There were lots of weekend visits to family and friends, even though most of them lived at least a three-hour drive away. Sometimes Bob didn't enjoy the visit and drove too fast on the way home. One time I was especially concerned about his driving and crawled into the back seat to sit between Ian's and Leona's car seats so I would be with them if anything happened. I probably should have done *something*, but I was just thankful to get home safe and sound.

We were usually able to connect with both of our families at Christmastime. Sometimes the weather was terribly snowy, making our mothers worry, but we still made the trip. The year that Ian was one year old, there was so much snow in Collingwood, where Bob's sister lived, that we had to leave the car parked at the end of their long country driveway.

Ian's cousins happily pulled him to the house on a sled. Our suitcases and other things went put on another sled. It was a fun adventure.

My parents' home in Hamilton was the family meeting place. My family came from Kingston, Mary's family came from Strathroy, and we all met in the middle. Clarence and his family lived in Hamilton as well, and they usually joined us. During the years that Len's family lived close by, it was a very full house at times. I still felt like I couldn't live up to my parents' expectations and often worried about how my children were dressed or how they behaved.

However, in time the blessings of time spent with my parents outweighed those negative feelings. When Dad and Mom visited they often helped with projects around our house, and sometimes Mom came for a few days so I could get some extra things done. Then there was a special visit when my mother gave me a booklet with words of encouragement and Scripture verses, titled *Who Cares When I Hurt?* Mom didn't say anything, just gave it to me. After my parents went home and I could spend some time alone, I allowed myself to feel my parents' love for me. So many lies the enemy had told me were washed away! Praise the Lord!

———

Camping was one activity that usually gave enjoyment to Bob, the children, and me, preferably at a site with water and electricity. However, there were no sites with hydro available when we went to Bon Echo Provincial Park, north of Napanee, Ontario, so we went semi-wilderness camping. We weren't too far from bathroom facilities, but we were quite isolated. Even in the evening when lanterns were lit and fires were burning, we were only able to spot one other occupied campsite. Though no big creatures seemed to be lurking about, I had no idea what wildlife I might meet when I ventured to the bathroom alone. We did have a wee guest one night. I have no idea how a mouse got up the steps and into the tent trailer, but I wasn't interested in having him join our family while Ian and Leona were sleeping. The chase was on! Soon the wee trembling critter was thrown outside, and we could get some sleep.

When Bob rented an apartment down the street from where we lived, the elders from the Fellowship suggested that I see a lawyer so I would be aware of my options should I need the information. I don't remember details of that time, but we must have been able to find some common ground, because Bob didn't move out, and we started attending Evangel Pentecostal Church together. Evangel was a friendly church, and it was less disruptive for our family to attend the same church. Soon the pastor's wife at Evangel was babysitting Ian and Leona when I was working on Wednesdays. I still worked at the penitentiary with one of the women from the Fellowship, so those friendships remained intact.

In the spring of 1985, Bob was having some challenges at work. He was asked to seek some counselling. Once again Bob said that the main stressor in his life was our marriage. This time, we found a Christian counsellor to go to. We were asked to say three nice things to each other every day, but I didn't find that exercise very helpful in our situation.

After a few visits together, we had final individual sessions. I was told that Bob would probably never change but I should continue on in the marriage for as long as I could cope. With God's help, I could cope, right? Somehow, everything was calmer again, as Bob had fulfilled the requirement for work.

Several years later I was talking to someone about our counselling experiences. He made me see how flawed that advice was. When giving the advice to "cope," the counsellor was more interested in saving our marriage than saving the people in the marriage. Trying to learn how to cope with unhealthy behaviour was not beneficial to any of the members of our family. How long could I cope? I tried to ignore that question.

Bob and I had been attending a local interdenominational Christian school's annual meetings as we intended to send our children to the school when they were of age. Because of our attendance at these meetings, we had stayed loosely connected to some of the friendships we had made at the Christian Reformed Church. These friends also sent their children to the school. I was surprised when I was asked to consider taking a term on the board of the school and even more surprised when I got elected to the position. I was blessed to know I was respected and appreciated by these people, another gift of light shining in my darkness.

By the fall of 1985, I wanted to work a bit more. The day I had my interview for a hospital position, I asked my neighbour Lil to babysit for me. When I got the job, I asked if she would like to babysit more regularly, and she told me that it would be an answer to prayer. She was an awesome "grandmother" and play partner for Ian and Leona. I was doubly blessed. I was working more and getting out more, and my children were having great fun with Lil!

I still worked my Wednesday job at Kingston Penitentiary and picked up other shifts in the critical care areas at a local hospital. We always seemed to be short of funds, as we were paying off our mortgage as quickly as we could. My extra shifts didn't help the stressful situations at home, though, as it was now more difficult to get away on weekends.

One of our Christmas cards in 1985 came from Bob's friends who lived in Langley, BC. They invited us to be their guests while we went to the world's fair, Expo '86. It was an exciting idea, and we decided to accept their invitation. For months before our May departure, I placed books, toys, and other items in a cardboard box in the guest room. By the time May arrived, Ian and Leona were very excited. The box was placed between their two car seats, and they could finally explore it and enjoy.

It was a *long* trip, but travelling went quite well. We stopped in Thunder Bay once again to visit with Margo and her family. We also stopped to see Bob's friend Dee and her family. It was good to spend time with Bob's friends in Langley and to enjoy their gracious hospitality. On a clear day they had a great view from their kitchen of Mount Baker. It was an awesome, majestic mountain that reminded me of God's great power and constant faithfulness.

We had purchased tickets for three days at Expo. We saw a lot of exhibitions and waited in many lines. It was great having small children with us. As we waited, clowns and acrobats and other entertainers came to entertain Ian and Leona as they sat quietly in their rented strollers. It made waiting so much easier for the adults as well. One evening we stayed for the fabulous fireworks and light show that ended each day. The highlight for me was visiting the Pavilion of Promise by Crossroads Christian Communications. It was a high-tech visual and musical extravaganza.

Our Expo trip was a good vacation. Driving across so much of Canada was a great adventure. On our return trip we did less visiting and more sightseeing. We had a lot of picnics as we travelled so Ian and Leona could run about during our rest stops. Near the end of our drive home I asked Ian and Leona if we should turn around and do it all over again, and they both said yes. Well done for a four- and three-year-old!

Once we were home, the realities of life had to be faced. Bob was still unhappy much of the time; I was still coping by escaping to work; we were still unable to figure out how to build a better life for each of us as individuals or as a couple. I was becoming overwhelmed by the challenges of my life. On July 28, 1986, I wrote a letter to my Father God and saved it, hoping that someday I would be able to rejoice in the changes we had made in our lives.

Dear God,
How do I go on from here? What's the next step? I know things can't go on as they are now. I have no room to grow. No one to build me up. I feel drained and defeated, except that I know You are carrying me. Oh God, when is Bob going to be able to see beyond himself? When are his needs going to be something I might be able to meet?

How do I go on by myself with the kids? Where do I get a job? Who looks after them while I'm working? I don't want to get to the point where someone else has to make decisions for me. I'm already finding it increasingly difficult to make any decisions about my life.

Bob says I'm responsible for Ian and Leona. He'll help me a bit, but that's all. I find that intolerable in our present situation. I'm staying here because of guilt and fear. There is no happiness. No sense of anticipation about the future. No sense of accomplishment or a job well done.

I was struggling to see the flicker that was burning in my darkness, but I was confident that God's Word is true. The light would not go out! I remembered my wedding text: "The light shines in the darkness, and the darkness has not overcome it" (John 1:5).

chapter seven

INTERLUDE I

Trust in him at all times, you people; pour out your hearts to him, for God is our refuge.

—Psalm 62:8

IN A FEW DAYS, OUR SITUATION DETERIORATED DRAMATICALLY. WE PLANNED to visit friends and Oma for the August long weekend. While Bob and I were in the process of getting organized for departure, we had a major confrontation of pushing, shouting, grabbing, and throwing things. Sadly, Ian and Leona were there. There had been another episode of pushing and shoving, and I was certainly not blameless. I had allowed my frustration level to get out of control. However, this time the children were witnesses, and I had a huge bruise on my upper left arm.

Immediately after, Bob left in the car, and Leona, who had been looking forward to our planned outing, went with him. I didn't know what to do. Ian and I went next door to visit with Lil briefly (poor woman!). Soon we were all back home, and somehow Bob and I came to the conclusion that we would carry on with our weekend plans. Leaving home and being with other people seemed like a good idea at the time. Unfortunately, I wasn't able to think about how our presence would affect the people we visited.

The bruise on my arm was clearly visible, and I wasn't practised at making up a story about how it happened. My friends were clearly uncomfortable after hearing what had happened. It was difficult for Oma to hear what had happened too. She cried. I don't remember if we received any words of wisdom or how we managed to spend time in the car together getting to where we were going and getting home again. I'm thankful for God's protection for all of us through all the turmoil. On the outside we were ignoring the situation, but on the inside, I was filled with more questions than I knew how to answer. So many times I'd heard women say, "If he ever hits me, I'll leave." Was it time for me to make a decision for myself and my family?

When I worked my next shift at the penitentiary, it was impossible to cover up my bruised arm. One of the doctors jokingly asked me if my husband had hurt me, and the devastated look on my face told the story. I knew then that changes were necessary. Bob and I were no longer coping with our life the way we were living it. I had asked God what the next step was, and now I knew. It was totally unacceptable for physical violence of that degree to happen between Bob and me, and that it happened in front of Ian and Leona was even more devastating. I insisted that a time of separation was necessary, and Bob agreed. Over the next weeks, I slept in the living room. This time I was leaving, to be close to family.

I decided to move to Strathroy to live close to Mary and her family so I would have some support when needed. I also thought it would be easier for my parents if I was a bit farther away from them. I no longer remember why I felt I needed six weeks to get Ian, Leona, and me organized to leave, but I planned to move mid-September. Soon Mary and Ed found a home I could afford to rent, and there was an indication that I would be able to get a job at the hospital there. Strathroy was a five-hour drive from where we lived in Kingston. I don't remember Bob making any comment about the distance, though it must have been difficult for him, knowing that his children would be so far away.

After talking to the kindergarten teacher in Kingston, I decided that Ian would attend school when it started, as he had been looking forward to the beginning of school. It was hard dropping him off at school that first day, knowing he would have to adjust to another school very soon. How would Ian and Leona cope with it all? How would I cope?

We made lists of household items and furniture and divided everything as equally as possible. I'm not sure I was consciously doing so, but it's clear now that I was preparing for this to be a permanent separation. I was not anticipating that necessary changes could happen.

On September 12, as I was driving to pick up the moving van, Psalm 37:4 came into my mind: "Take delight in the LORD, and he will give you the desires of your heart." I was totally confused. I asked God how I could be getting the desires of my heart when this separation was happening in my family. My desire had been to be a wife and mother, and what was happening, though necessary in my mind, hadn't been part of *my* plan. I'd had dreams of having a welcoming home, happy husband and children, and cooking, cleaning, canning fruit, freezing vegetables, making jam and pickles, working a bit as a nurse, and being of service to my community. My life seemed to be taking me in a very different direction. However, I felt God near me as I made that huge step into an unknown future for me and my children.

The men from the Fellowship came to help me get the moving van loaded, and my father and brother Clarence came from Hamilton to help with the driving. Ironically, the day Ian and Leona and I left Kingston was our sixth wedding anniversary. That evening a convoy of three vehicles drove from Kingston to Hamilton. Clarence drove the van, Dad drove his car, and I was in my car with the children. After staying in Hamilton overnight, we drove on to Strathroy the next morning.

Ian, Leona, and I moved into a yellow brick house that I rented from a welder whom Mary and Ed knew through church connections. Dad and Mom, Ed and Mary, Clarence and Jeri and I all worked together, and by evening, a truck full of furniture and other household items had been moved into a home for Ian, Leona, and me. I was very appreciative of all the love and support but very lonely, and I felt a huge weight of responsibility on me. I was going to have to move forward "inch by inch."

One evening Ellie, whom I hadn't seen since high school, arrived at my door with her husband, looking for the welder who owned the house. It was a reminder of the threads in the tapestry of my life that God is creating.

After our arrival in Strathroy I applied for a job at the local hospital and made plans for childcare for Ian and Leona. I also had an initial appointment with a divorce lawyer, a woman, who tried to get me as angry and riled up as possible. She wanted Ian and Leona to have psychological assessments done for "greater leverage" in our favour. I saw her one time and didn't return. Being angry and riled up was certainly not a route I ever wanted to take purposefully.

Very soon—*way too soon*—Bob's mother asked us to see a marriage counselling couple she had found near Strathroy. Keith and Patsy were known to have a 100 percent success rate. It was a difficult time for me. I couldn't find a reason for refusing to go, but I didn't feel ready for marriage counselling either. So two weeks after I arrived in Strathroy, when Bob came to visit the children, we also went for counselling together.

During our sessions with Keith and Patsy, we each did a personality profile and then compared the two profiles to help us understand our relationship better. Through the profiles I was able to see more clearly how Bob and I interacted. I tried harder to change myself to meet Bob's needs. In that discussion, we talked about my "nursing personality." As a student nurse, I had been praised for my ability to deal with a sad situation in one room and switch to a happy situation in the next room. During counselling sessions I was told that most people can't switch their feelings that easily. My "quick switch" could make Bob feel like I didn't care or I was ignoring his feelings. Later, during difficult times, Bob often mentioned my "nursing personality."

In counselling with Keith and Patsy, the focus was once again on saving the marriage and not on saving the people in the marriage. Some sessions were brutally difficult for me. There seemed to be a lot of extra support for Bob. I felt confused and hurt and more negative about myself than I ever had. Later, Keith explained to me that he had used that approach so Bob would continue coming for sessions. It was more than twenty-five years after those sessions when I recognized and believed that most of those comments that had hurt and made me feel negative about myself were only intended to try to convince Bob to remain in counselling. They hadn't really been about me.

Soon I started working in a casual position at the local hospital. Several registered nurses on the medical unit were on maternity leave, and there were lots of available shifts. God was providing for our needs. I was earning enough money for our living expenses and for Christian school tuition. Ian, Leona, and I were coping quite well.

During those first months in Strathroy, Bob was still living in Kingston. Four weeks after our counselling sessions started, Keith and Patsy suggested that Bob and I go away for a weekend together. It didn't feel right, but I didn't say I didn't want to go. We started sleeping together again.

Keith tried to have private sessions with Bob, but that failed. After three or four months of couple's counselling, I had a private session with Keith. He told me that I should continue in the marriage as long as I could cope. *Really? Again?*

Bob and I convinced ourselves that keeping our family together was best. We decided to sell our house in Kingston and reunite our family. I tried harder to change myself to become the wife that Bob needed. I felt that the opportunity for me to grow stronger as a person was gone. I was very confused, but my trust in God stood firm.

chapter eight

MARRIED—THE STRATHROY YEARS

"So do not fear, for I am with you; do not be dismayed, for I am your God. I will strengthen you and help you; I will uphold you with my righteous right hand."

—Isaiah 41:10

IN THE SPRING OF 1987, OUR HOUSE IN KINGSTON SOLD, AND BOB WAS ABLE to move to Strathroy permanently. It was a good time in our lives to live closer to family and friends. Mary's older children were able to babysit for us, and we attended the same Christian Reformed church they did. There were several people in Strathroy that I knew from my younger years in Forest and Sarnia, including Helen, who had been my best friend in grades 1 and 2. Bob was able to connect more easily with people from his youth too. It gave us a sense of belonging that had been missing in Kingston.

Bob didn't have a job initially, but I was getting enough shifts at the hospital to pay the bills. We were able to purchase a semi-detached home, near the hospital and along the bus route to the Christian school that Ian attended. I enjoyed being able to walk to and from work. It was good to be in our own home again. In our vegetable garden I had another chance to plant seeds and watch things grow.

Soon after his arrival in Strathroy, Bob met Ken, who gave him occasional projects to do. Bob set up a work bench in the basement and did some work from home. These were challenging times for him. Eventually he got a full-time job in the nearby city of London, but he didn't enjoy it. He felt that his prospects for getting a job he enjoyed were limited.

At the hospital, several staff who worked in the intensive care unit quit their jobs. This created more full-time nursing positions. We decided that I would work full-time and Bob would start his own business.

He was usually home for Ian and Leona when I was working, so our childcare expenses decreased. I had never anticipated working full-time while my children were young, but it seemed to be the best decision for our family.

I worked twelve-hour shifts. I couldn't spend much time with Ian and Leona after I came home, at 7:15 p.m. or later, and it was also sometimes very difficult to sleep during the day. However, I had more days off than some working mothers have, which was an advantage with a busy young family. With twelve-hour shifts, I only worked seven shifts every two weeks. This didn't give me more energy than other people who worked full time, which was an easy thing for Bob and me to forget.

——

One day I got a survey in the mail that the Christian Reformed church sent randomly to me. It had various questions on abuse in marriages. As I read the questions and selected my answers, I realized that I had been in an emotionally abusive marriage when we lived in Kingston. Now I felt that I had gained some control of my life, and things were better. Bob no longer had the stressors of a job he didn't like, and we were doing more things together. Ian and Leona were a bit older, and we had fun family outings, too. Soon life was too busy for me to evaluate my marriage or change how I was coping with stressors in my life.

When we bought the semi-detached house in Strathroy, we hoped that we would soon build our dream home. A property down the road from the Christian school was divided into lots, and we bought a corner lot, across from where soccer fields would be eventually. It was farther from work for me but closer to Mary and her family, and it had good highway access to the city of London should more frequent trips be needed in the future. The fun of selecting a house plan started. In the end, with the help of a draftsman, we modified some plans we had seen and made them our own. We wanted to have a workshop for Bob's business that would be a bit separate from family living. We had our plans, but it would be some months before we could start to build.

One summer Sunday in 1987, my father experienced cardiac arrest while he was in church. Fortunately there were trained people in attendance at the time, and his life was spared. While Dad was in the hospital, we quietly took Ian and Leona in to see him, one by one. They saw their grandpa briefly, got a peppermint from him, and were relieved to see that after all the scary stories they had heard, Grandpa was still okay. After we got home, Leona said, "We'll be lucky when we die because Opa [Bob's father] has been in heaven for a long time. He'll have lots of peppermints for us when we get there." It was precious to hear my child's thoughts.

In the fall of 1989, the uncle and aunt whom Bob had lived with as a wee lad told him they would give him a trip to the Netherlands as a birthday gift. We were unable to afford a ticket for me, as we hoped to start building our house the spring of the next year. They decided to pay for my trip as well and wanted us to feel free to visit my relatives too. It was great for us to be able to make the trip together. Bob's uncle and aunt still lived in the same house they had lived in all those years ago. We also visited the cemetery where Bob's father was buried and saw the places where he had lived and walked to school. I enjoyed all our visits on both sides of the family.

Once we were back home, house selling and building and planning details were all-consuming. Our house went up for sale in February of 1990, and it sold in a month. We now had a deadline. Many supplies were bought, which would have to be moved to the new place too. When we bought our lot, the agreement included a clause that the exterior of our home had to be completed within six months. We decided to have a contactor do the exterior and the framing of the rooms. Bob planned to do all the plumbing and electrical work himself. We would work together on the rest of the interior. It was a *huge* project.

Initially, after construction started, it was possible to see progress every day. Slowly our ranch-style house with a porch on the front was emerging. It was exciting, but there were so many decisions to make. As soon as possible, Bob started doing electrical and plumbing projects so we would be able to live in the house when we needed to move. Our main focus was to have a usable bathroom in the basement so we would be able to camp out in our own house. Meanwhile, all our things in our other home had to be packed up. It was a very stressful, busy time, as I was working full-time and Ian and Leona sometimes needed help with schoolwork.

When we moved, we put our sofa bed and two twin beds in one basement room and made that our living space. Our fridge and stove were set up in the kitchen space, and we had managed to complete the downstairs bathroom. It was quite a fancy campsite. In a few days our washer and dryer were hooked up. We had figured out how to live in our space. Some family members helped put in some insulation and put up drywall. All our initial inspections went well, and Bob got high praise for his plumbing and electrical work. We were only able to contemplate building this way because of the skills Bob had. For a season, his job was working on the house.

Ian and Leona don't remember the house-building years as a bad time. Ian was a bit sad when the drywall was put up for the ceilings as he enjoyed climbing into the rafters to read a book. Leona liked the spaciousness of the unfinished house. I didn't let the fact that the house was "in process" stop us from having family in or having birthday parties for the kids. We lived life as normally as possible.

That summer we got away from our campsite home for a while. We rented a cottage near Kingston and took Ian and Leona on a tour down memory lane. We went to places they didn't remember that had been a part of their lives: Old Fort Henry, the Thousand Islands, and the house we used to live in. At the cottage, we rented a boat and spent some time on the water. One day, when Bob and the kids went out on the water, I stayed at the cottage alone and then felt guilty for missing time with my family. I was recognizing that I needed some "me" time but wasn't sure how to make that happen.

During the first years of our marriage Bob had managed our incomes. He worked full time and I worked part time. Some of our money went towards paying off our mortgage as quickly as possible, but there seemed to be times when there was no money left for the last week before payday. After our reconciliation, when we lived in Strathroy, I became more involved in managing our finances. I needed to know that there would be money for class trips and other unexpected expenses.

When Bob was setting up his own business, the list of things he needed seemed to be endless, and I sometimes wondered if all the equipment and parts that were stocked in our basement were necessary. Aside from that, we lived quite frugally. When we bought living room furniture, the material on one armrest of the couch was visibly flawed. I planned to make something to cover that up but never seemed to make the time. Even though I had much, I often felt like a "poor person."

On February 3, 1991, my father had his seventieth birthday. He gave each of his children and grandchildren an awesome gift. With Mary's encouragement and help, he wrote his autobiography, which he titled *A Life of Grace and Blessings*. Other treasures from Dad are the wood carvings he did after he retired. It was a special Christmas when Dad gave each of his children a carved loon. He only did one hardwood project, an eagle, which he said was the right gift for me. "Those who hope in the LORD will renew their strength. They will soar on wings like eagles; they will run and not grow weary, they will walk and not be faint" (Isaiah 40:31). It was a blessing to know that Dad recognized strength in me that I often wasn't able to feel.

In July 1991, Oma had her seventieth birthday. I wanted to have a surprise open house birthday party for her. We had a deadline to work towards for some of our house projects. The kitchen cabinets were installed and the floors were painted, as there was no flooring. Before the party, I painted most of the rooms and wallpapered some walls. The trim was missing everywhere, and there were still many other projects that needed completion, but on the day of the party, it looked like a livable space. We got several comments about how spacious our home was. It wasn't a large house, but we had been very careful to use the space we had to our best advantage. I'm glad we were able to have the open house. Oma's friends, neighbours, and relatives dropped in by invitation. It was a fun day as Oma was very surprised about the people we had invited.

———

Because of our lack of skill, we had hired a drywall contractor to finish the walls and ceilings. However, we decided to mud, tape, and finish the drywall inside the closets ourselves as that wouldn't be too visible. One day near the end of Desert Storm, part of the war on Iraq, I was using a sander in a closet. I suddenly thought about how absurd life can sometimes be. There were Kurds in Iraq trying to stay sheltered from the cold, wind, and rain with a piece of plastic, and I was worrying about how smooth my walls were inside a closet. My father often said, "The more you have, the more you have to worry about." I had *so much,* and worrying about the inside of a closet seemed a bit ridiculous. However, if I viewed our home as God's gift to us, it was important to do the best job I could on the projects I tried to do.

After the initial necessary work was done to the house, Bob once again put more energy into his business. He did projects for various people and companies. Some weeks were busy. Some weeks were slow. He became more involved in church and Christian school committees. We had a large garden in the summer, and there was always yard work or snow shovelling to do too. These were busy years without much time for self-evaluation. I didn't recognize that I was falling into the same patterns I had been in before our separation.

The following weeks, months, and years were frustrating, as the finishing projects on the house seemed endless. There were long periods when little building work was being accomplished. I worked full time and took care of the housework and the yard. I often had very little energy to spare. I had been told to stay in my marriage as long as I could cope, and I convinced myself that I could cope with the endless job list, too.

My relationship with Bob hadn't improved. We weren't communicating better, and I still had very stressful times of trying to be sure that Bob's emotional needs were being met. I felt it was necessary to try to meet his need for intimacy as well. Bob would sometimes want to talk long into the night, and I wouldn't get the sleep I needed before work the next day. At times when we argued, I would start crying and go to our room. When I was able, I would dry my eyes, get up, and carry on.

Through the busyness of my life, I continued the practice of reading my Bible daily. Bob usually did his devotions in the evening as well. For a while, we tried to pray together. It was unfair, but as I poured out my heart to God, I was able to say things that I wasn't able to say directly to Bob. Soon he no longer wanted us to pray together. I didn't find another way to share my feelings with Bob and seldom shared them with anyone else.

———

I had worked full time for five years before the principal of Ian and Leona's school realized that I was a full-time working mother. I tried to help with hotdog days, attended assemblies, helped with school trips, and went to field days as often as possible. I traded shifts when I could to get the time off to attend events. Ian and Leona both played soccer and had swimming lessons in the summer. They ran on the cross-country team at school in the fall. Attending these activities was an opportunity to sit quietly outside, interacting with other parents.

I was fortunate that most days I enjoyed my job at the hospital and the people I worked with. In the early days, much of our patient care was done by "doing rounds." We started at one end of the unit as a group and did the care that was needed for each patient as we went from room to room. The group interactions with nurses and patients were enjoyable, and there was often much laughter. It was great to be in a place where I was appreciated and accepted. Sometimes, an unexplainable deep well of joy would rise up from somewhere. God's provision through a full-time job added stressors to my life but also many blessings.

We were camping at Wheatley Provincial Park on July 1, 1992, when Canada celebrated its 125th birthday. We drove to Windsor, Ontario, to join in the celebration at the Windsor–Detroit International Freedom Festival. The fireworks that evening were amazing. On the following Sunday we attended a church in Wheatley. It was a communion service: the Lord's Supper was remembered. Ian and Leona were invited to attend children's church partway through the service. When they rejoined us afterwards, Ian and Leona excitedly told us about their experience. They had been asked if they loved Jesus, and when they both said yes, they were invited to join the other children in communion. This was different from what was practised at our church, but as their mother I was very pleased that Ian and Leona had made a profession of their faith and participated.

In March of 1993, I became quite ill. My doctor ordered some blood work. Just as I was leaving her office, I started crying and said I felt like I was dying. She added thyroid tests to those she had already ordered. I thank God for those tears, because my thyroid was not functioning as it should. The initial plan was to see if my thyroid function would return to normal, and it did. However, in the fall the same problem presented itself, and I needed to see an endocrinologist. He wanted to test my parathyroid gland as well. I was upset because I recognized that stress was a big part of the problem. I felt like I was destroying myself. I didn't seem to know how to make changes in my life. I didn't take the time or have the energy or opportunity to take care of myself. Hopelessness and despair were setting in.

I put a lot of energy into trying to make our lives appear normal on the outside. It actually wasn't too hard, as the abnormal part was hard to explain. It seemed to be more about how I felt than about an incident I experienced. Family activities were a part of "normal." Day and weekend trips as a family were important. We went to Blue Jays baseball games, Niagara Falls, African Lion Safari, the Canadian National Exhibition, and other events and visited family and friends.

The abnormal part was that many of our activities and outings were because of Bob's need to socialize and go to places of interest. In some ways it seemed like he was trying to live as he had in his single days, but now he was taking his family with him. He often took multiple photos with frequent lens changes, and he read many plaques. It often kept me from enjoying the outings fully. Sometimes Ian and Leona got impatient too, and it took energy and ingenuity to keep them entertained. Also abnormal were petty little incidents that seemed unimportant when taken individually, but added together over time, they sucked the joy out of situations.

———

Some good things can't be taken away or spoiled! February 14, 1994, was my fortieth birthday, a day that was celebrated with my extended family. Ed and Mary made a huge red heart to which they attached forty balloons. The heart was so large that the waving balloons could be seen from the parking area in front of the school that Ian and Leona attended, which was a block away. I'll admit that the attention was fun! I kept the heart for many years. In a different home, the heart had a special place of honour hanging over my workbench. It was a nice feminine touch.

One of the best decisions we made was to add a puppy to our family. Sydney (Syd), part Australian shepherd, joined our family when he was about six weeks old. He had been born on February 2, 1994. Birthday cakes for Syd became one of our family traditions. He soon loved all of us, and we loved him back. When it was time for Ian and Leona to come home from school, Sydney would come from wherever he was and lie down by the door to wait for them. There was an awesome reunion every day! Syd changed our lives.

A fun outing for all of us, including Syd, was to go to the big sand dune at Port Franks. My parents, siblings, and I had also enjoyed time there. Syd, Ian, and Leona enjoyed using up their energy on the dune as much as we had. One time, Syd patiently allowed Bob, Ian, and Leona to bury him in the sand except for his head. Syd was happy as long as he was with his people. For me, it was so peaceful to be up at the top of the sandy hill with the breezes, the views, and the soft, warm sand. I always had to be cautious going down the sandy hill, though. It was quite easy to start going too quickly in the deep loose sand and lose control. So much fun!

—————

One day in March of 1996, I had a wonderful Christian woman as a patient. We were able to share a little about ourselves. The next day, she handed me the wee corner of an envelope. On it, she had written "Dear Annette—thanks for being such a wonderful nurse. Be encouraged in the Lord. Jeremiah 29:11–14 and Isaiah 58:11. I really sense this is for the whole family." I printed those verses out on cue cards, and they were posted on our refrigerator for a long time. Over the years, those verses have been a blessing to me again and again. At some point I forgot that she felt that the promise of those verses was for my whole family. I was glad to be reminded of that when I found her original wee note in a plastic sandwich bag in my box of treasures in the summer of 2012.

"For I know the plans I have for you," declares the LORD, "plans to prosper you and not to harm you, plans to give you hope and a future. Then you will call upon me and come and pray to me, and I will listen to you. You will seek me and find me when you seek me with all your heart. I will be found by you," declares the Lord, "and will bring you back from captivity."

—Jeremiah 29:11–14

"The LORD will guide you always; he will satisfy your needs in a sun-scorched land and will strengthen your frame. You will be like a well-watered garden, like a spring whose waters never fail."

—Isaiah 58:11

Later that spring, I needed the promises of those verses. Bob was increasingly unhappy. He was on the council at church but didn't feel respected by some of the men. It made Ian and me uncomfortable around those men as, unfortunately, Bob discussed his feeling with Ian as well. I found myself purposefully avoiding them because I didn't want to let it slip that I had talked to one of them. One day in the grocery store, I skipped an aisle and came back to it later as I had seen one of the men shopping there. I wasn't even thinking about how ridiculous this behaviour was. It was easiest to avoid confrontation.

Bob's business hadn't progressed as well as he had hoped it would. We made the decision that he would go back to college in September and update his education. I prayed that this would help Bob feel better about his life. Soon another challenge presented itself. In April, I lost my fulltime position. I was given the option of working casual part time in the intensive care/cardiac care unit (the unit) or being laid off. For a while I had switched places with a nurse who worked on the unit for two weeks every three months, so I had already had an orientation. God had prepared me for such a time as this. I took the position.

Working in the unit wasn't the biggest challenge. It was working with no schedule, without a secure number of shifts. I was glad that there were usually several booked shifts. I worked any day, any time, often on short notice. There were short shifts and trips to London in the ambulance. It wasn't easy, but the options were few. However, since I also lost my benefits, the hourly pay was better because I got "in lieu of benefits" paid out.

I felt that I would probably be able to get enough shifts for us to meet our financial obligations. So even though were we still paying tuition fees for Christian school education, we decided to stay with Bob's "back to school" plan. We decided that Bob would take out student loans but we would pay for as much of his schooling as possible from my income. We would save as much of the student loan money as possible.

In the summer of 1996, Dad and Mom celebrated their fiftieth wedding anniversary. During a visit to Canada the previous summer, Dad's twin brother had asked Mary if she thought it would be possible for us to include all of Dad's siblings and their spouses in the celebrations. Four couples would visit from the Netherlands for two weeks. My parents knew that my father's sister planned to come, but the others would be a surprise. It was an exciting idea, and my siblings and I were determined to make it work. It was the push Bob and I needed to finally have flooring and carpets installed.

Mary and I didn't want to shock Dad and Mom too much, so we repeatedly told them that we had a *big* surprise planned. On the day of the surprise, we all eagerly awaited the arrival of my parents, Dad's sister, and her husband. Our uncles, their wives, and a few of our children waited inside as Mary, Ed, Bob, and I sat out on our front porch. Mary said she felt like she was pregnant and the baby was finally going to be born. It was a funny but very appropriate comment. We had been preparing for this day for almost a year.

When Dad and Mom and their guests arrived, my parents were reminded again that there was a *big* surprise inside. What followed was pure joy! My parents thought that Dad's twin brother might have come again, but they never for a minute suspected that the younger set of twins and their wives would come too. I doubt that any of us who were there will ever forget the joy of that evening. It was great for me to see Dad and all his siblings together.

Meanwhile, my parents had one final surprise in Hamilton. My siblings and I had paid for our brother Len's flight to Ontario from BC so he could join the festivities as well. It was our anniversary gift to our parents and a gift they enjoyed more than anything else we could have bought for them.

I kept a journal about all our plans and preparations for the anniversary celebrations. It included the year-long process of getting ready, the two weeks that our Dutch relatives were in Canada, and the anniversary dinner and open house. My uncles and aunts also wrote their thoughts, in Dutch, in the journal, and I gave it to Dad for Father's Day that year. It was a treasured gift. Mom said she cried when she read it because she was so deeply touched by her children's thoughtfulness in getting everything organized. It was a blessing to be able to honour Dad and Mom through these celebrations.

In August, Len returned to Ontario with his family. It was an opportunity for Dad and Mom's children, grandchildren, and a few "soon to be" family members to spend a week at a cottage on Lake Huron. Bob was working that summer and wasn't too interested in joining the extended family events. After the initial weekend, Bob returned home and to work. My parents planned to take a family picture on the last Saturday, but Bob wasn't sure he would come back for the photo session.

I talked on the phone with Bob a few times during the week, and I was getting increasingly upset. I wanted him to be in the photo. I tried not to talk about it with the others as it was a very happy week for them. After some pleading on my part, Bob arrived on the Friday evening. The fiftieth anniversary family picture was taken the next day, and Bob was included.

Later in August, we had opportunities to spend time with Bob's extended family. One of Bob's cousins had immigrated to Canada the year after we got married, and his two oldest daughters were getting married a week apart. Bob's aunt, two of her daughters, and two grandchildren came from the Netherlands for the celebrations. We were delighted to have them all come for an overnight visit. Bob and I attended both weddings and saw other members of Bob's extended family, most of whom I had met before then. These were enjoyable events. I thought it was good for Bob to have this time with his family after he had struggled to feel included with my family.

There had been other challenging times all through our marriage, but in hindsight I can see that something changed after that busy "family" summer. Bob started having long conversations on the phone with his friend Dee, who was now divorced again. If talking to a friend helped him feel better, I was all right with that. It was also becoming increasingly difficult for me to spend time with my extended family as it seemed to be a contest in Bob's mind: him or them. All of this was subtle control and perhaps not consciously done on Bob's part. I often felt like I was on a battleground, but I didn't understand the battle or who the enemy was. I continued to believe that God would make things better in His time. The light would shine in the darkness, and I would have the desires of my heart.

In the fall, Ian was in his second year at a private Christian school in London, Leona was in grade 8 at the local Christian school, and Bob was driving to London each day to go to college. I enjoyed the quiet when I was fortunate enough to be home alone. However, in January of 1997 a big change happened in our lives. Leona started a cycle of migraines that lasted days, weeks, months, and years, and she still has frequent headaches. It was life-changing for her and affected all of us. It was heartbreaking to see her suffer, and I felt helpless. She was seldom able to attend school and missed most other activities. By completing her core subjects at home, and with Mary's help with French, Leona was able to graduate from grade 8 with her peers.

There were several "armchair quarterbacks" in our lives at that time; some gave good advice, and some said very painful things, as they felt Leona's symptoms weren't real. I think we all have areas of our lives where we feel our opinion matters even though we don't have enough knowledge to make a good judgment. Bob's comments and actions often offered little support. Leona worked hard to take control of her life. She took ginger instead of Gravol so she wouldn't be drowsy; she worked hard to figure out what her food triggers were; she refused to give up on running and soccer, as she wanted to remain active. Many days the migraines won, but I was, and still am, proud of her fighting spirit. *Leona* means "courageous." "Be strong and courageous. Do not be afraid; do not be discouraged, for the LORD your God will be with you wherever you go" (Joshua 1:9).

The summer of 1997, we rented a Boler trailer to pull behind our van and took a trip to the east coast. We saw beautiful scenery as we drove east towards the coast. Our drive had been quite hilly in the eastern United States and continued to be so in New Brunswick and Nova Scotia. It became apparent that our van was having difficulty pulling the trailer. One dark evening on a hill in Nova Scotia, after we heard lots of noises from under the hood for a while, our van suddenly stopped completely at the top of a hill *in the middle of the road*. Bob accepted the offer of a ride with some people to get help. Ian, Leona, and I waited anxiously in the van, unsure if we were safer inside or outside of it. Later, a tow truck driver parked the Boler trailer at a campsite for us. Our van needed a new transmission.

We rented a car for a few days of sightseeing, but the trip remained stressful. Bob had trouble coping with the reality that Leona had headaches. Also, he had been to the east coast before and knew all the places we "should see." On previous family vacations, Ian and Leona had been young, and Bob had made many of the decisions about where we would go and what we would do. This time, Ian and Leona were in their early teenage years and had ideas of their own about how they wanted to spend their time. We saw lots of beautiful scenery, drove the Cabot trail and went to the Fortress of Louisbourg. Through it all, I was constantly trying to keep peace in the family. It was not a great family vacation.

———

When Mary's daughter, Heather, was planning her October 1997 wedding, she asked me to be the hostess at her wedding reception. I was honoured that she asked me. However, Bob didn't want me to participate. This time, I didn't give in. It was another event that should have been filled with fun and excitement, but there was too much tension for that. The control that had been subtle before was beginning to be expressed in words.

A short time later, I read a booklet put out by the Back to God Hour that contained a printed sermon titled "The School of Hard Knocks" by Rev. David Feddes. It included a list of poor coping mechanisms: dishonesty, short-sightedness, anger, and wishful thinking. When I read that list, I realized that I was no longer coping in a positive way. I was using every negative coping mechanism listed to survive my marriage. In my state of coping poorly, recognition of the problem did not result in action.

In July of 1986 I had written, "I don't want to get to the point where someone else has to make decisions for me. I'm already finding it increasingly difficult to make any decisions about my life." Years later, I didn't recognize how broken I had become.

During the years of our marriage, Bob and I had gone away together, on occasion to Florida or to the Netherlands but usually overnight or for a weekend. These times seemed to help hold our marriage together. Our times away were about meeting physical needs more than our communication needs, but I felt that was important too. In February 1998, Bob wanted to attend a one-day conference in London and asked me to go with him. I don't remember anything negative about the day, and I enjoyed the connections with people I saw there. However, the next day...

chapter nine

INTERLUDE II

When I said, "My foot is slipping," your unfailing love, Lord, supported me.

—Psalm 94:18

On Sunday, February 8, 1998, Bob rented a U-Haul trailer and announced to Ian, Leona, and me that he was packing up his belongings and moving to Alberta to live with his friend Dee. It was a pivotal moment in my life in that I began to understand that it was time to allow God to do a new thing in my life, to cleanse me and renew me. I had gotten lost and confused, tired and despairing. It was the beginning of an ongoing journey of learning to love myself. Outward changes didn't happen immediately, but deep inside I was different.

On that Sunday, I couldn't figure out what I should do. Ian and Leona knew that there was a trailer in our driveway, and I could no longer ignore my situation. I don't remember where Bob went, but I needed to talk to someone. We had started attending the church down the street, and Bob was an elder there too. The first thing I did was walk to the church to tell our pastor what was happening. He promised to come to our home after the afternoon service.

When I returned home, Ian, Leona, and I went for a walk in the soccer fields across the street. They told me that they wanted me to allow Bob to do whatever he wanted to do. They didn't want me to try to convince him to stay. Later, our pastor and an elder from the church arrived. Bob and I sat down together with them and agreed to seek marriage counselling at the first opportunity.

Our first marriage counselling session with Karl was on February 16, 1998. Karl said he could see love and strength in our relationship. I was sure I wanted to have more sessions, as I knew I needed change. Bob and I had become too good at hiding the pain we were experiencing in our lives. I had stopped talking about my feelings long before, and it was difficult to open up in an initial meeting with someone. We attended two more sessions with Karl together, and then, with my approval, Karl met with Bob alone.

Before our next joint session on March 22, Bob found out that he would be able to try out for a specialized repairs job at a hospital on March 24. He had gone back to school so that he might have such an opportunity. I thought life would be so much better for Bob if he got that job and was earning money again. The possibility of that job was on my mind when we sat down for our next joint session with Karl. In my mind I can still see Karl before he started speaking. When he looked at me, he was wringing his hands and had a sad but determined look on his face.

He then told me that it would be best for me to get out of the marriage. We talked about the many phone calls Bob made to Dee, some of which I had known about. Karl wondered if I even cared about the marriage any more. He said that we should have a separation and not consider having more marriage counselling until Bob got the help he needed personally. If his counsellor told me that Bob was ready for marriage counselling, then we could pursue that again. I needed to have counselling too.

Karl reminded Bob and me that no marriage is a mistake when there are children involved. God has a purpose for their lives. It was a comment that I remembered many times over the following years and reminded Ian and Leona of, too. God intended Bob to be their father and me to be their mother. Our only choice is to trust Father God, trust His purpose, and trust His plan. We have a Father who loves us more than we can ever imagine.

During that counselling session, my mind was going in many different directions at the same time. If Bob had a job when we separated, life might be less complicated. It was Monday. Bob's opportunity to try out for the hospital job was on Wednesday, and I wanted Bob to go. I doubted he would attempt the job if we separated that evening, so I said I wanted to keep trying to make things better in our present situation. Karl was taken aback but gave us an appointment for the next week.

There was much for me to think about after that session. I realized that on some level I had admitted defeat long ago. I had spent years making sure I would be able to survive if our marriage failed. But part of me had still thought that God would change our marriage into something better at some point, maybe in our retirement years. The light would shine in the darkness (see John 1:5), and I would have the desires of my heart (see Psalm 37:4). Now, however, I had to accept that, with God's help, I needed to change how I lived my life *now*. Changes in me might help all of us.

The tough question I had for myself was "How has this happened to me?" Several years before, I had realized that there had been emotional abuse in my marriage during our years in Kingston. My situation was worse now than it had been then. Recently, I had recognized that I was coping by using dishonesty, short-sightedness, anger, and wishful thinking. I was dishonest with myself about my own needs. I was short-sighted and used wishful thinking when I thought that Bob and I would magically have a better relationship someday. I buried my anger towards Bob and covered it with thinly veiled resentment. I had recognized these negative things, yet it hadn't propelled me into making changes. Why not? How had this "abnormal" way of living become "normal" for me?

I knew that Karl was right. Bob and I needed to take separate paths to healing. I talked with my dear neighbour Fran, who was an awesome support. In God's perfect timing, Fran had recently listened to a radio segment about how to be sure you have a Christian counsellor. She took extensive notes and shared those with me. It was a blessing to compare Karl to the list and feel confident in following the advice he gave. I was now 100 percent sure that I would need to tell Bob something different than I had said in front of Karl.

Bob came home after his trial day at the hospital pleased with how well it went. He told me that he would be going back the next day. This was a huge relief for me. I could no longer keep my silence, and I told him I had lied to him when we were with Karl. I was no longer prepared to continue with our marriage.

Bob returned to Cambridge the next day, and things did not go well. He didn't get the job. He visited some friends on his way back to Strathroy, and when he came home later in the evening he told Ian that he would be moving to Alberta the next day. Ian came to tell me Bob's plans.

I cancelled my shift at work the next day so Bob and I would be able to make some decisions about our home and our finances before his departure. We made a document and both signed it; this later led to heartache and confusion because our agreement wasn't legally binding and many things needed to be changed. I don't know if Bob ever fully intended to leave, but he didn't go to Alberta. Later that morning, I went to Mary's home alone for the first time in eight and a half months. It had been easier to not upset Bob. I had learned ways to keep life as peaceful and calm as possible.

Our pastor met with us once more. Even though we'd had marriage counselling as requested, he still wanted to try to save the marriage. It was a difficult session for me. I don't remember what was said, but I remember that I walked out of the room at one point. After our pastor left, Bob said, "Now you can't talk to him anymore either." This was the first and only time Bob gave me a *direct order* not to talk to someone. I was surprised, but I recognized that I wasn't meant to be controlled in that way. Shortly after that visit, Ian and Leona asked me to speak to our pastor, requesting that he stop trying to fix the marriage.

———

Initially, Bob was still at home and didn't seem to be making plans to leave. He didn't recognize that this time I wasn't going to go to our room and cry and later come out when I could carry on. He slept in the guest room, ate his meals with us, and joined us on walks with Syd, our dog. It was a stressful, confusing, boundary-less situation for Ian, Leona, and me. After a few days, Bob left for a visit with Pastor Chris. His absence was a welcome relief from all the awkwardness.

Shortly after Bob left, a dozen beautiful red roses were delivered. They were from Bob. This was not normal behaviour for him. What should I do with these beautiful flowers? First I hid them behind a chair so I would only look at them when I planned to look at them. Then I thought about giving them away, but who would want the roses I had received in these circumstances? I wasn't able to come up with a better solution than to throw them into the garbage. I can still picture myself dumping the rose blooms into the garbage can first, so all I could see were the thorny stems. It felt like a victory.

We still had one marriage counselling appointment set up, so at my request, Karl met with Ian and Leona. He asked them to make up a list of "rules" for Bob and me. These rules would be discussed at a family session on a later date. After Karl spoke with Ian and Leona, he also met with me for a few minutes. He was surprised at how much better I looked physically. Wow! It was hard to imagine that hope could make a change happen so quickly. I was ready to change, to begin taking care of my own needs. I was thankful that we had a counsellor who cared about the people in the marriage.

Karl and I talked about emotional abuse and emotional adultery. My personal "normal" had become "abnormal." I was no longer being true to my own values. I had built a protective shell around myself, and I coped by living in my marriage but no longer caring about it. Karl reminded me that Bob and I each needed to have personal counselling first and marriage counselling later, if God should lead us there. He gave me the courage to look at the future. Karl was a special gift to me during that very difficult time.

While Bob was still gone, I bought a devotional book for single parents. The first reading I read was from Psalm 68 where God promises to be "a father to the fatherless, a defender of widows" (Psalm 68:5). I found a new husband, helper, and defender that day. I had felt alone for so long. I also started writing in the first of many journals. I wrote, "My idea of the future has changed so drastically. I know God has a plan for my life and that I'm living part of that plan now! Praise God. I don't have to understand it."

———

My family did their best to support me during this time. Bob later said that it was my parents' acceptance of divorce that was the problem. I remember best a conversation with my brother Clarence. He told me not to make the same mistake of the past. He felt I needed to wait a long time and be sure of change before I ever considered getting back together with Bob again. When my mother told Ian that he had to be the man of the house now, I gently told both of them that Ian would always be my son first. Mary seemed to feel the need to be more in my life now that I was alone. I don't think she realized how alone I had been for a long time already. God protected our sister hearts through our challenging times.

Bob phoned me while he was visiting Chris. I told him that our current relationship was over, and we needed to see if God would lead us into a second relationship after counselling. Our courtship had been very brief, and we would need to fall in love before we considered re-entering a marriage relationship. We also talked about Bob's relationship with Dee, which he was unwilling to give up. While Bob was on his drive home, Chris called me. It was good to talk with Chris, who had become my friend too.

———

On Sunday, April 5, when Bob wasn't in church, the announcement was made that because of family difficulties Bob would no longer be an elder. I don't remember much else except that the three of us (Ian, Leona, and I) were sitting in the middle of the centre set of pews about two-thirds of the way back, and we sank into each other in a puddle of misery. Getting out of the church was difficult, and I'm quite sure that other people didn't have any idea of what to say or do either. I don't know if I had been warned that the announcement was going to be made, but I certainly wish we hadn't been there. Church definitely did not feel like a safe haven to any of us that morning.

———

Soon after Bob's return from his visit with Chris, it became clear that it was too difficult for Ian and Leona to have both parents living in the same house under the circumstances. I shudder when I think of what those weeks must have been like for them. Bob packed up some of his things and went to live with his mother until he could make other arrangements. This wasn't an easy time for either one of us. Neither of us had a clear picture of where we were going or what we were doing, but staying as we were was no longer an option. I realized, however, the power in Karl's comment that we had to fix ourselves before we would ever be able to fix our marriage.

I borrowed a book from the library, *On Your Own Again: The Down-to-Earth Guide to Getting Through a Divorce or Separation and Getting on with Your Life,* by Keith Anderson and Roy MacSkimming. I read that the first 100 days are the toughest because of sheer loneliness, and I marked off the first 100 days in my journal. The book also mentioned four stages of recovery. For me, the timing of the stages was very different from what the book said, but the progression was the same.

Would I have the strength, courage, and patience to deal with the future challenges? God had so clearly shown me His presence in my life. I had to move forward trusting Him.

chapter ten

ON MY OWN AGAIN —HURTING

I will give you hidden treasures, riches stored in secret places, so that you may know that I am the LORD, the God of Israel, who summons you by name.

—Isaiah 45:3

TWO DAYS AFTER BOB MOVED OUT, THE FOUR OF US MET WITH BRUCE FOR OUR family session to go over the list that Ian and Leona had made. Among other things, it included the following: Bob should move to Alberta if he would be happiest there; Ian and Leona would get to hear our stories from each of us; Ian and Leona could choose which parent they wished to live with, and Sydney would live with them; Bob and I could both attend special ceremonies involving Ian and Leona; and Bob and I would not live in the same town.

It was good for us to know their wishes. Some items on the list surprised me, but I was glad that they had the opportunity to create the list together. Long ago, I hadn't wanted Ian to be an only child. I was now blessed that my two children supported each other, and I was thankful for Karl's guidance in this. Ian and Leona have had to remind me of this list a time or two, and it has helped guide me in the right, agreed-upon, direction.

———

I had no idea how hard the separation would be for me. I had thought there would be a sense of relief, but there wasn't. It was just an awful big *ouch*! I had to deal with the loss of my marriage and my status as a wife. My family had become a statistic, a broken home. People I hardly knew asked too many questions, and I gave too many answers. Somehow I felt like I had to explain my situation, like I had to justify the choice I had made. I really didn't know if these people were collecting gossip or if they would be praying for me and my family.

During the first few weeks of adjustment, the words of Zephaniah 3:17 were very true for me: "In his love he will no longer rebuke you, but will rejoice over you with singing." I would put six CDs into the player, set it on "random," and be blessed by God's timing. I would kneel in front of the big chair in the living room and allow the tears to flow as I allowed the truth of God's love to wash over me. One particular song especially blessed me; it wasn't until several years later that I realized that I had misunderstood the words. I had heard what I needed to hear, not what was actually there. In the stillness, in the quiet, He was there.

Through times of emotional chaos I wrote again and again in my journal that I had "escaped" to the garden. In the garden, good and positive things happened. Bad weeds were pulled, and order came from chaos. It was good to see order and growth. One evening as I was writing in my journal, I came across a quote that reminded me of the words from Nehemiah 8:10 "the joy of the LORD is your strength." I was amazed, surprised, and delighted that in my present circumstances, I still experienced joy.

Mary Southerland said it so well in her Girlfriends in God devotion "Choose Joy":

> Joy is not the result of outward circumstances. Joy is an inside job, a deeply rooted confidence that God is in control. Every trial or loss, every defeat or victory measured against this confidence can be counted as joy...We cannot avoid pain but we can avoid joy. Our inward perspective does not have to reflect our outward circumstances. The pursuit of joy is a matter of choice.[2]

With God's help, I found the strength and energy to do what was necessary for survival.

---

2 Mary Southerland, "Choose Joy," Girlfriends in God, January 26, 2016, http://girlfriendsingod.com/choose-joy/

This was an exhausting time for Ian and Leona as well, both physically and emotionally. I was still sorting through so much in my own life that I did little more than meet their basic needs. Ian was having difficulty getting his schoolwork done, and Leona continued to have frequent headaches. Sometimes I came home after a twelve-hour shift and bought fast food for their supper. Sometimes they slept too long in the morning and I drove them to school after working a night shift. There were many days when one or all of us didn't feel well. However, walking Syd with Ian or Leona in the quiet of the evening was always a positive way to end the day. It was a time of great conversations and quiet reflections.

In the weeks that followed, Bob continued to be at the house frequently when he visited with Ian and Leona. Most of his belongings were still in the house, as he had nowhere else to take them. He saw Keith and Patsy again, this time for some individual counselling. They asked Bob's permission to see me alone to assess how they should proceed, and they asked me if I wanted to proceed with marriage counselling. Bob's response to our situation was to once again seek marriage counselling? My answer was no, just as I had already told Bob. Keith and Patsy then recommended a lawyer, a man they were confident would represent me well. He was a huge blessing to me in the months and years ahead. He kept us out of court, and his support helped me make choices I can look back on without regrets.

I realized that the support I got from my church family would have been very different if I had lost Bob through death. The cards I got from some individuals meant a lot to me. Some people stopped by when I was doing yard work and just listened. One young man had a business nearby and drove by our house often. He always looked to see if I was outside and waved to me if he saw me. Those waves meant a lot to me! And when

I had to replace my car, my church brothers at the auto wreckers were very helpful.

I was deeply hurt by a joint decision made by the council of my church, though. Bob and I had a mail slot at the church with both of our names on it. I asked if we could have separate mail slots. I didn't want the painful reminder of "my failure" as I went in to worship. My request was denied. The council members felt that it would signal that they had given up on our marriage. They refused to make changes until a divorce was final. For a few months I stopped attending that church and went to a local Baptist church.

> Some divorces are wrong. Some are necessary. All are to be mourned. No one knows that better than those who have been there. Such persons don't need our condemnation. They need others to join them in grieving lost love and broken dreams.[3]

At the end of May I was still counting down my first 100 days. I wrote, "Thirty more days to go. It doesn't seem possible that life will feel anywhere near normal by then." Bob and I had initially agreed that Ian, Leona, and I would be able to stay in the house until Leona was finished high school, but Bob seemed to be changing his mind. I met with Brenda, a real estate agent, and I also had the first meeting with my lawyer. Brenda told me about a couple hosting a Divorce Care group. I was very interested in that. The visit with the lawyer wasn't as positive. It was hard to hear about how our assets would be divided. A big difference for me was that I had a pension plan at work, and Bob did not. The benefit for me would be later.

Over the past few months, other people had noticed changes in me, but now I began to notice the restoration of my health, physically and mentally. Towards the end of the marriage, I was too short of breath to take long walks (I'm not exactly sure why). Now, when Ian, Leona, and I took Syd for a hike in the conservation area, I tolerated the exercise

---

3 Herb Vander Lugt, *God's Protection for Women: When Abuse Is Worse than Divorce* [Grand Rapids, Michigan: RBC Ministries, 2005], 13

well. Bob and I had initially talked about remaining friends, but that hadn't been possible, because there wasn't enough trust between us. I was pleased that I was able to cope with going to a track meet that Ian and Leona wanted both Bob and I to attend and that we were all able to have lunch together.

Shortly after we separated, Ian told me that he hoped to do the Ontario Ranger program that summer. It was hard to think about him being in northern Ontario for seven weeks, but I couldn't ask him to stay home. Leona was confident that she would be able to stay at home alone with Syd the nights that I worked. The 100 days of sheer loneliness after Bob left and the seven weeks that Ian would be gone were going to overlap for a while. Added to that, Leona often spent lots of time in her room because of her headaches. The loneliness was confusing for me. In many ways, I was relieved that Bob was gone, but this change was still so hard.

That summer, I was still working part-time in the unit. There were many quiet shifts, which were difficult as I had too much time to think. Between work and home I had too much quiet. I was glad when it was time for my vacation. First Leona and I went camping at Sauble Falls, which has a wonderful beach. We also tried playing tennis, but I tripped over my own feet, and Leona laughed at me. It *was* funny! Our next stop was Miller Lake to spend time with my parents and members of Mary's family who were at a cottage there. It was good for us to be away from home and enjoy time with family. We had left Syd at a kennel but were quick to pick him up on our return.

During Ian's absence Leona went to visit Bob at his cousin's farm and brought a kitten home. She named the six-week-old kitten "Shadow." After Leona's visit, I drove to the halfway point to meet Bob for the transfer of daughter and kitty. I tried to talk to him about how disrespected Ian and Leona felt because when visits were planned, he didn't pick them up when he said he would. He also wasn't reliable about when he brought them home. Bob became angry—end of conversation.

On August 14, Leona and I left at 5:35 a.m. and drove to the northwest corner of Algonquin Park, where Ian had spent the last seven weeks. On the drive home, Ian told us lots of stories about his adventures. He had enjoyed his experience. When we arrived home at 8:30 in the evening, I was very tired and felt ill, depressed, and discouraged. The joy of Ian's return was not as visible as it should have been. I wrote, "I love Ian and Leona very much and want to be the best I can be for them. Help me, Lord! It is good to have Ian at home. We will adjust." My first 100 days of separation were over, and Ian was at home again. God reminded me often of His love for me, and I was blessed by that. However, after ignoring my emotions for a long time, I was starting to feel again. I was hurting.

When Ian got home, he met the newest member of our family. It was interesting watching the initial interactions between the new kitten and our dog. Syd was not allowed everywhere in the house, and Shadow soon figured out where to go to get to a safe place. The kitten would run down the hallway towards the laundry room. It was a good spot for Shadow to turn around and look at Syd just standing there, not moving forward, as he wasn't allowed in that part of the house. A good, obedient dog and a smart kitten made for a fun combination; they were soon great friends. Our pets were a gift from God to all of us.

I began to make adjustments in how I spent my money. Bob had put an antenna of some sort between the rafters of the house, so we had been able to get some TV channels. But now we once again had cable TV, just like during our first separation. Ian and Leona were able to watch many more sporting events. Also, rather than sitting in the "nosebleed seats," I bought tickets for good seats at a Blue Jays baseball game in Toronto. There was even a special event for us to see that day. We watched Roger Clemens end his shutout innings streak at thirty-three, a Jays' record at that time. It was a fun outing.

———

In the quietness of my room one August evening, I read Isaiah 43:18–19: "Forget the former things; do not dwell on the past. See, I am doing a new thing! Now it springs up; do you not perceive it? I am making a way in the wilderness and streams in the wasteland." It was like a hug from God. I needed to be reminded that I couldn't fix my past. God was in charge of my future, and I had to trust Him. I needed to reread that verse often.

Towards the end of the summer, I started counselling sessions through the employment assistance program at work. I was asked to make a list of all the hurts during our marriage and to work on self-acceptance. The list of hurts was long, and it was painful to think of all of the events and then to make them real by writing them down. I realized that many of the things I was writing I had never shared with anyone. I recognized that some of Bob's actions that I had accepted as "normal" had actually been hurtful. I had been ignored in many situations. While writing the list, it was also necessary to forgive myself for my part in all of it, for not speaking out in defence of myself when hurtful actions happened.

Self-acceptance was slow in coming, and it would be a long process. After one counselling session, I wrote, "I'm slowly feeling freer and less embarrassed by my situation." Could I learn to focus less on the breakdown of my marriage and more on the healing of my own emotions? Healing was essential, no matter where God was leading my life. Soon the counsellor suggested that I had the tools to move forward and that it would be best not to make counselling my crutch. I was comfortable with that, as Divorce Care was starting soon, and I felt I would get any added support and direction I needed.

On October 10, 1998, Tim, Mary's oldest son, got married. It was an out-door ceremony in the trees across the street from where we lived. I was asked to help with setting things up before the ceremony, which I gladly did. It was fun to be involved. It felt different being at the wedding as a single person but nice that I didn't have to be concerned about Bob's feelings or behaviour. Ian, Leona, and I joined my extended family at the reception. A highlight of the evening was watching my father dance with the bride's uncle (both sober, just being lovingly goofy!). It was a fun celebration.

In mid-October, Bob decided he wanted the equity from the house *now*! I wrote, "Even though I thought I had prepared myself, I was very upset." During the months since our separation, I had adjusted to living in limbo and had been ignoring the changes that still had to be made in our living situation. I needed to "unstick" myself and start making plans.

Ian's and Leona's visits with Bob often didn't go well. It was difficult to hear their disappointments and frustrations. I wrote, "I have difficulty talking to Bob without getting angry." Working together to make decisions about selling the house might be challenging.

When my marriage ended, it hurt more than I could have imagined. Some healing had started through "hidden treasures, riches stored in secret places" (Isaiah 45:3). There were many random touches of God's love: music, working in my garden, and guidance as I made decisions, like buying a car. I had to remember that the only way to walk the road in front of me was to walk it with God. No one knew my heart or the circumstances like He did.

Learning to *be still* was an ongoing process. Years later, I wrote to a friend, "I've learned that 'not thinking' is a protective gift from God. I think it helps us get over the physical parts of the stress we've gone through without interference from the mind. In time, the thoughts will come and you'll be better able to handle them. Enjoy the calm—it is a gift from a loving Father!"

chapter eleven

ON MY OWN AGAIN—EXPLORING

I waited patiently for the LORD; he turned to me and heard my cry.
—Psalm 40:1

LATER IN OCTOBER 1998, DIVORCE CARE STARTED. I LEARNED MANY LESSONS, which I will share later. After the first evening, I wrote, "I found it very helpful and am looking forward to next week." The next day, I was deeply hurt, and it was good to know that I would be at Divorce Care again the following week. While Ian, Leona, and I were eating supper, I answered a knock on the door. I had to sign for an envelope, which I discovered contained a divorce petition. It hurt that Bob had not warned me that he had taken this step. The contents upset me as well. After looking at the document, I told Ian and Leona that I had to talk to Aunt Mary and Uncle Ed. When I left, I told them I would be back soon.

After a discussion with Mary and Ed, I decided that Ian and Leona would be allowed to read Bob's document if they wished to. They were in their mid-teens and deeply affected by all that was happening. During our family session with Karl, Bob and I had agreed that Ian and Leona would be allowed to hear our versions of the story. This was Bob's version of our story with his signature on it. Ian read it; Leona didn't. I don't remember all that was written as, fortunately, I only had the document for a very short time.

There are two things I *do* remember. First, the statement that I had only been interested in advancing my career, not in what was best for the family, and, second, that I could have full custody of Ian and Leona. Both statements were hard to read. I was blessed that I liked nursing, but

I certainly would have liked to have more time for my family and home-making. I wasn't sure how to interpret the custody issue, but somehow it felt wrong for Bob to choose to be uninvolved to that degree.

——————

October 23, 1998, was Ian's seventeenth birthday. In June 2012, when I read about that day in my journal, I cried. I was overwhelmed just reading all that had happened that day. First, in the morning I went to London to meet with my lawyer. I had received the divorce petition two days previously. I left the document with him and never saw it again. Since I didn't contest the divorce, none of those issues had to be dealt with. However, the main purpose of my visit was to deal with Bob's request for financial support. From financial statements that had previously been done, the amount I should offer Bob was $150 per month. My lawyer explained that this was a better option than going to court, for both financial and emotional reasons. I agreed even though part of me wondered if my life would be easier if I worked less and wasn't able to give support. .

Later that morning, I went shopping for a gift that Mary would give to Ian for his birthday. I dropped it off at Mary's home on the way back to my house. After lunch I went through our house with Brenda, the real estate agent, to prepare the listing for the sale. After Brenda left, I had a short nap and then got up to go to the grocery store to get a special after-school birthday snack. Mary came to drop off Ian's gift while we were having our snack. Later, Ian, Leona, and I went to Pizza Delight for supper and then went to play three games of bowling. So that day I handed over my divorce petition document, agreed to spousal support, went shopping, worked on the listing for the sale of our house, napped, and celebrated a birthday. I wasn't done yet.

At the end of the day, I went to work at 11:00 p.m., until 7:00 a.m. the next morning. I slept in the morning. After lunch, Bob came, and with Brenda's help we signed listing papers for the house. Later, Bob, Ian, Leona, Syd, and I went for a hike as part of Ian's birthday celebration. It was a beautiful day to be outside, with all the sights, smells, and sounds of fall. I walked quietly most of the time. At the end of the day I was tired, but I wrote, "I felt good about the day." I was civil to Bob. I didn't break any promises to the kids. So many emotions and so much activity packed into two short days. It was good that after so much stress, I was satisfied with myself.

For quite a while after our separation, I had fleeting moments when I wondered if it would be possible for Bob to rejoin Ian, Leona, and me. It seemed it might be easier to have our family go on together instead of each of us needing to figure out a new path. However, each and every time those thoughts came into my mind, God reminded me of some obvious brokenness of the past and helped me face the necessity of a new future. "Leave the broken, irreversible past in God's hands and step out into the invincible future with Him."[4]

———

After Ian's birthday, my life had a new busyness. Between October 28, 1998, and January 14, 2000, when the house finally sold, there were twenty-nine house showings and five open house events. I think Ian, Leona, and I can be proud of our willingness to leave the house on short notice so often, especially when Ian and Leona were in school. One day, Leona called me at work to ask if it was okay if there was a house showing later that afternoon. I told her that she and Ian could decide if they had time to get the house ready. Wow! Great kids! The busyness definitely impacted how we lived our lives during that time.

During the years of my marriage, our family hadn't developed good routines about chores because I didn't want to ask my children to do things I wouldn't ask their father to do. I did too many things myself. It wasn't the best for any of us, but that's how it had been. Now, I was blessed each time Ian and Leona helped me when they had the time and energy. The house showings made it necessary for us to learn these lessons. Every cloud has a silver lining. One Saturday, I wrote "surprise me" on their list, and they did. When I opened the garage door at the end of my work day there was a big "SURPRISE" sign across the garage space.

---

4 Oswald Chambers, ed. James Reimann, *My Utmost for His Highest* [Grand Rapids, Michigan: Discovery House Publishers, 1992], devotion for December 31

It was good when I could see some fun and laughter coming back into our home.

———•———

Just before Christmas I attended a "Ladies Night Out" event with my new Divorce Care friends. I wrote, "It was an enjoyable evening. I saw many people I knew, but I didn't go to talk to anyone. *That must change.* I must make myself available to people." It wasn't uncommon for me to be cautious in new surroundings. It saddened me to realize that I was uncomfortable around people that I had been comfortable with for years. A few weeks later, I wrote, "Many people are telling me I seem more relaxed and happier. Hopefully I will soon be able to notice the changes too."

My first Christmas as a single mother I was disappointed to find out that I had to work a twelve-hour day shift on Christmas Day. On December 22, I wrote, "Tonight Ian, Leona, and I had our Christmas dinner, and the kids proposed one toast after another. Many were very beautiful: expressed much praise and thanks." I wish I had written down what some of those things were.

Ian and Leona spent Christmas Day at Mary's home with my extended family. They probably hardly noticed my absence, which was a good thing. My brother Clarence didn't want me to spend the whole day without family, so he came to have lunch with me in the hospital cafeteria. I wondered if anyone would say anything about my male lunch guest, but Clarence and I are obviously related, so we started no new gossip.

———•———

After Christmas, my life settled into a quieter routine. Our real estate agent told us to sell the house "as is," so I no longer worked on house projects. Ten months after our separation, I finally had time to go through photos and the filing cabinet to separate items Bob should have from items I should have. I noticed that I had very few photos with Bob and Leona in them. I also noticed as I went through phone bills that Bob had called his friend Dee more often than I had been aware of. Many of the calls must have been after I started working at 7:00 p.m. For two years, he had called Dee on or near our anniversary and my birthday. Suddenly, Bruce's comment about emotional adultery made more sense to me.

———

Since the previous October, I had been attending Divorce Care, which had a huge impact on my life. I felt an acceptance at our meetings that I wasn't able to feel elsewhere at that time. The "focus verse" of the first lesson of Divorce Care was Jeremiah 29:11: "'For I know the plans I have for you,' declares the LORD, 'plans to prosper you and not to harm you, plans to give you hope and a future.'" I was again reminded that I could feel hopeful about life. Divorce Care gave me a lot of information but also made me look for my own answers.

After we discussed forgiveness, I wrote, "I was really blessed as I thought about forgiveness. I know God helped me a lot by making me realize right away that I couldn't fix the old relationship." The mistakes of the past no longer mattered. I asked Bob to forgive me for any part I played in the breakdown of our marriage. I also sent Dee a letter, as Bob had initially planned to move to Alberta to live with her. In her response, Dee told me that she had been in another relationship for six years, and Bob knew that. She wasn't sure where the confusion came from. In my journal, I wrote, "I was angry, hurt—I cried, threw clothes around." Had Bob purposefully misled us about his relationship with Dee? After much thought, I shared that information with Ian and Leona. Leona was especially grateful as she had been angry with Dee and she could now let go of that anger.

One of our Divorce Care leaders reminded us often that "vengeance belongs to the Lord." It almost gave me the feeling of watching to see how God would punish Bob. I wasn't comfortable with that. I have since found a verse that describes how I felt. "The LORD will fight for you; you need only to be still" (Exodus 14:14). I wanted to know that God would fight for me, for the changes that needed to happen in me. I wanted God to fight for changes in Bob, too. It was best to "be still" and watch God at work.

There was one huge challenge for me from Divorce Care. Our leaders talked about biblical divorce. In their thinking, divorce is only valid if there is sexual immorality or abandonment by an unbeliever. I certainly didn't want to be outside of the will of God. One of the leaders said that she was sure Bob would soon find another woman and I would have a valid reason for divorce. I didn't like the idea of wanting and waiting for Bob to "do wrong," and I certainly didn't feel I had the right to judge his relationship with God.

One Scripture that helped me was Matthew 18:15–17. These verses explain the steps to take when having a conflict with a fellow believer. The first step is to talk to the person (Bob and me), then to talk in front of witnesses (marriage counsellors), and then with the church (pastor). Those steps had been followed without resolution of our marriage problems. Whatever I recorded about my feelings after reading those verses has disappeared in multiple scratches in my Bible.

In Divorce Care, we were told not to expect a quick fix of our damaged emotions. It was suggested that emotional healing would take one year for every four years of marriage. After more than seventeen years of marriage, I could anticipate more than four years of "finding me." At that time, that seemed like a *long* time, but I discovered that I needed those four years—and more. There were some factors that contributed to the length of time I needed. Our "uncoupling" wasn't an easy one, in more ways than just our emotional bonds.

———————

On my own, in the privacy of my own room, I worked through *Violent Voices: 12 Steps to Freedom from Verbal and Emotional Abuse*, by Kay Marie Porterfield. The book explored the dynamics and effects of being in an emotionally abusive relationship. There were exercises based on the twelve-step program that helped me explore my childhood and made me feel better about myself. It was a *very* worthwhile process. I discovered five areas of weakness. Some areas have improved more than others. As I allowed God to change me, acceptance came, and I set better boundaries in my dealings with others.

My Five Areas of Weakness/Challenge

1. Being too nurturing: I took care of Bob and my children in ways that prevented them from doing things they should have been responsible for. I got worn out and resented it.

2. Being too encouraging: I encouraged Bob even when I thought what he wanted to do wasn't the best in the situation. I didn't confront and challenge him even when it might have been beneficial for him.

3. Feeling too easily rejected: Rejection had been a challenge before my marriage, but the years of my marriage only compounded those feelings. I became very sensitive about anything negative that was said around me. It made it hard for others to help me once I started seeking help.

4. Not sharing problems: Lack of communication was a major problem. I tried to cope with many situations when I should have shared the burden. I needed to allow someone else to walk with me through my struggles. I felt that Bob wouldn't even try to "be there," so I avoided rejection by not sharing my problems with him. I should have reached out to others more.

5. Being the victim: My life could sometimes be a big pity party. I had been hurt by Bob, and life felt better when others supported my feelings. This prevented me from moving forward and was a lesson not easily learned. One year, Leona asked me to rewrite our Christmas letter as she felt it was too much of a "pity party." I recognized that she was right.

Shortly after the end of my marriage, my parents moved to Strathroy. They sold their house in Hamilton and bought a two-bedroom apartment in Trillium Village, a seniors' complex. Dad and Mom gave me some of the furniture they no longer needed. This was very helpful, as

Ian, Leona, and I were still using some furniture that would eventually be Bob's. I moved more of Bob's furniture downstairs.

One of my Divorce Care leaders said that I was still allowing Bob to control me by the things he still had in the house. It was uncomfortable at times with him coming and going at will. He didn't live close by, so it didn't happen often, but it was still disruptive. Then, at some point, I became concerned enough about Bob's behaviour to have the locks changed. I wrote, "It would be so much easier if the house would sell—but God doesn't seem to think I should have the easy way out." My frustration with God's plans never stopped Him from showing His love to me!

I started to dream about what our new home would be like. I wrote, "Wish list for *our home*—close to the hospital, 3–4 bedrooms, family room, one good-sized room for family gatherings, central air conditioning—under $92,000." One day when Mom was going for a walk between the seniors' complex and the hospital where I worked, she saw a semi-detached home for sale that she thought would be ideal. Ian, Leona, and I went to see the home. It was ideal, but it was "for sale by owner" and I was quite sure I didn't want to try to figure out all the details involved on my own. Also, the price was too high, there was no central air conditioning, and our other house was still for sale, so the timing wasn't right.

———

At the beginning of 1999, Ian and Leona were still attending a private Christian school in London. Leona's headaches were still a daily part of her life, and the forty-five-minute bus ride made school days more difficult. After the first semester, Leona and I decided that she would switch to the local high school. Her headaches continued, but she was able to attend school more often. In the spring, at Ian's request, Bob and I attended his grade 12 graduation supper together. We ended our time together by taking pictures of Ian with each of us. After the supper I joined Leona and members of my extended family to watch the graduation ceremony. It was great to see Ian reach this milestone in his life.

When school started in September, we were still doing house showings regularly. Now both Ian and Leona were attending the local high school. At that time the fifth year in the Ontario secondary school system still existed, but the courses weren't offered at the Christian high school Ian had attended. They were soon involved with the cross-country team. In spite of the busyness it brought, being involved in sports was very good for our family. Running was a great stress reliever and benefited them, mind and body. It was good for Ian and Leona to have the responsibility of self-care so they could compete well. I attended as many games and events as I could. It was a simple, fun way to have family time.

Leona's years of playing soccer ended in 2000. For thirteen years I had been attending Ian's and Leona's soccer games on summer evenings. I missed the interactions with the other parents and the conversation time with the kids in the car when a game was over.

———————

My lawyer and I had already decided that I would not contest the divorce, so all I had to do was sign a statement of agreement. Emotionally, it was a struggle to ignore the things Bob had written in the divorce petition, even though I couldn't remember much of it. It was definitely best to just move forward! Five weeks after I signed the papers, a letter arrived in the mail. On June 16, 1999, the divorce judgment was granted. In thirty-one days, on July 17, the divorce was final. I sent a self-addressed stamped envelope to the courthouse, and my divorce decree arrived in the mail in that envelope. The divorce was final, but the matrimonial home still had to be sold, and the financial settlement still needed to be done.

———————

A close friend and I sometimes went for a walk. It was always good to get the exercise, and I probably wouldn't have made time for a walk without an invitation. My friend listened to all my hurts and frustrations. Sometimes she made random comments about divorced people that I found very hurtful. After one especially hurtful conversation, I was blessed that my dear neighbour was outside and noticed my distress. She was God's gracious provision. My friend later explained that she wasn't thinking about me when she made those comments as she didn't think of me as a divorced person. Unfortunately, that explanation wasn't helpful.

Another time she expressed major concerns about Ian and Leona and the way I was parenting them. I knew that sometimes trying my best might not be good enough, so I felt guilty about that. I also felt guilty for not appreciating my friend's way of expressing love and support. No one really understood what I was experiencing. It was a lonely time. I wrote, "I almost feel overwhelmed with things that are beyond my control—but God can control the universe, and He is in control of my life, too."

———

The summer of 1999, I was working, and Ian and Leona were both at home all day. The previous summer Ian had avoided thinking about our family situation by going north. Leona had worked very hard to complete her school year. A summer without pressures would be good for both of them, I thought. I was still in the beginning stages of my own recovery and unable to give Ian and Leona the support they needed, but I didn't always recognize that.

One evening, when Leona and Syd came back from a walk, Leona came in the front door instead of through the back gate. She told me that a man had started talking to her and then followed her. She hoped he didn't see which house she went into. I wasn't overly concerned, but then our back neighbour knocked on our door to ask if Leona was all right. He had noticed what was happening and had called the police. I found Leona crying in her room and felt terrible. I had dismissed her concerns too easily.

Another evening, Ian and I were walking with Syd. One property had a wooden fence to keep in three angry loudly-barking dogs. Suddenly, the gate popped open. The dogs ran towards Syd and started attacking him. Ian was down on the road trying to protect Syd, and people came out of their homes with baseball bats and golf clubs. The dogs were eventually restrained, but not before Syd had a few bites on his neck and Ian had scrapes on his legs and arms. The police were called, again. Ian and Leona were upset that I hadn't let Syd run free sooner, but that hadn't been my first instinct. After Ian was on the ground, my focus was on him. Of course, Ian's response was that he would have been okay.

Incidents like these were stressful. Our neighbourhood had always felt like a safe place; now I wondered what would happen next. Also, Ian, Leona, and I usually supported each other in a crisis, but now they were both quite upset with me. It was a very lonely feeling. Parent, child, friend, helper—sometimes they were helping me; sometimes I was helping them. Mistakes were made, victories were won, and somehow we each muddled through it.

It was good when God provided some "adult time" outside of work. That summer, Mary and I had our first "sisters' outing." We went to see a play at a summer theatre and then out for dinner. We enjoyed ourselves so much that we tried to make a sisters' outing a yearly event. Over the years, Mary and I went to plays, explored small towns, or took longer trips. On our longer trips, we circled two of the Great Lakes. On some levels, Mary and I had very different life situations, but we equally enjoyed these outings.

———

One sunny fall afternoon, I drove Leona to a cross-country meet in Wingham, a town a two-hour drive from Strathroy. While we were there, I had a full-blown panic attack. There had been warning signs leading up to this. I sometimes woke up at night feeling panicked and short of breath. It scared me, but after I realized that my symptoms were anxiety driven, I could control them.

However, while I was at that cross-country meet, I suddenly got a feeling like I was going to die. Leona had already started to run. I wanted to leave a message for her, so I went to look for her coach to tell him what was happening. I have no idea what I planned to tell him. Fortunately, I didn't find him. Eventually I was able to calm myself enough to sit on the grass under a tree and think more clearly. By the time Leona was finished her run, I was able to drive home without incident. I knew I had to get antianxiety medication that I could use when I needed it.

By October 1999, one and a half years after he left, Bob's situation was more secure. Fortunately, he had only needed spousal support for a few months. He bought a house and came to get the furniture that we had decided would be his. The living room was mostly empty, but there was still furniture in the family room downstairs. There was also still construction garbage downstairs. I bought a skill saw so I could cut up all the extra lumber in the workshop and clean it up. I tried not to think about whether it was fair or not that I was cleaning up the mess. Doing something felt like progress, and I needed to see progress somewhere.

At the end of 1999, the world braced for chaos. Would computer systems crash when the calendar switched over to 2000? Would our clocks be affected? Would there be days of great inconvenience? There was a lot of talk about how we should prepare for the possibility of disaster as 1999 became 2000. I usually had our pantry well stocked, so I didn't make much fuss about getting prepared. A new century started without incident. There were no problems at all with the "Y2K bug."

On January 11, 2000, I wrote,

> Dear God…Who am I really? No longer a wife—too busy to be a good daughter or mother, too burned out to be a good nurse or friend, too isolated, downtrodden, depressed to feel joyful.
>
> I feel overwhelmed with sadness sometimes—like there's no point in going on.
>
> Are Ian and Leona really okay? Did I do the best I could?
>
> God! I need You! I need to yield control of my life to You! I need to trust You to take care of us.

I always feel You can't bless me unless I do more—but there's nothing I can do that would make me deserve Your care and love. It's grace—underserving love.

You love me as I am right now—tired, sad, and broken.

Help me to be willing to stand firm, dig my heels, and not keep sliding back. I don't know or understand Your purposes and ways, but they are perfect—help that to be enough.

Help me to become what You want me to be.

Right now, I'm Your tired child who worked nights last night—got up to do a house showing at 2 and needs to work 19–23 tonight,

Rest—Come unto Me all ye who are weary and heavy laden and I will give you rest.

Awesome God! Within days of my desperate cry, there was action on the sale of the house. Bob wanted to switch real estate agents if the sale didn't go through, so I was hoping and praying it would. Brenda, our real estate agent, had worked hard. Praise God, on January 20, Ian, Leona, and I watched from the front window as Brenda put the "SOLD" sign in place.

God had an awesome surprise in store for me. Brenda had just added the semi-detached home we had looked at in the summer to her listings. It had been August 6, 1999, when we first saw the house on Maple St. The price was higher then, and I was concerned that it had no air conditioning. By now I was no longer paying Christian school tuition and had been able to save some money. Paying the new asking price and getting air conditioning was a viable option.

Mary and Ed helped me tour the house again. On January 22, 2000, I put a conditional offer on that house. It was a very crazy, stressful, exciting forty-eight hours: one house sold, and I made an offer on another house. By January 31, all the conditions for the sale were met, one of which was that the owners would find another home that suited their needs. Moving day would be March 24. "God's voice thunders in marvelous ways; he does great things beyond our understanding" (Job 37:5).

The new house was amazing for us. Dad and Mom's apartment, the high school, and the hospital were within walking distance. It met all the criteria on my wish list and more. It had a built-in dishwasher, a fenced yard for Syd, a workshop complete with workbench, a good-size shed in the backyard, and a patio by the side door. The laundry/utility room was the whole width of our house and could serve as Syd's indoor space when we were all out. The church that Mary, Ed, and my parents attended was very near too, and we soon attended there again. Only God could have found this perfect spot for us and orchestrated how these events unfolded.

As I was busy preparing to move, I got a notice that I had to appear for jury duty. I was excused after I sent in a photocopy of proof that I would be moving soon. And, just to keep life interesting, sometime during all this excitement I got the news that I'd been named in a law suit at the hospital. Several other nurses and a couple of doctors were also named. I've discovered that sometimes it's a blessing to have too many things happen at once. I could have gotten caught up in all the anxiety some other nurses were feeling, but I didn't have the time or energy for that. Eventually we met with the hospital lawyer and then the lawyers representing the patient. Later, the case was settled out of court.

———————

I was tired the morning of moving day as I had worked until eleven the evening before. I wasn't as prepared as I had hoped to be, and I panicked for a few minutes. However, with Dad, Mom, and Mary helping, we were ready for the movers on time. By mid-afternoon, Ian and Leona were able to get Syd and Shadow from the "old" house and move them to our new home. The next day there were twelve people, family and friends, working together to help Ian, Leona, and I get settled into our new home. A few weekends later friends came to help me paint the living room and dining room. It was a blessing to be able to receive all this love poured out on my family of three.

Even though it was a good move, living in our new home was a tough adjustment. I was feeling insecure, I was feeling overwhelmed, and I was feeling very lonely. I had to face the reality that I really was on my own. I was the sole owner of this house. The care and maintenance of it were my responsibility. When I bought my house, I got a mortgage and a line of credit until the money from the sale of the matrimonial home was freed up. I had mortgage payments and loan payments each month.

On May 12, I wrote, "Still no word from the lawyer re finances. Have to start paying taxes in July, so hopefully all will be settled by then." I continued to pick up as many shifts as I could. I was working many weekends and sometimes three different shifts within a week. I was feeling *very* tired and burned out. It was probably a good thing that I didn't know then what I know now. It would still be a long time before the money from the house was released. I began tithing during this time because I knew I should. God provided throughout. When asked how I was surviving, I would say, "The jar of oil is never empty!"

Then the word of the LORD came to him [Elijah]: "Go at once to Zarephath in the region of Sidon and stay there. I have directed a widow there to supply you with food." So he went to Zarephath. When he came to the town gate, a widow was there gathering sticks. He called to her and asked, "Would you bring me a little water in a jar so I may have a drink?" As she was going to get it, he called, "And bring me, please, a piece of bread." "As surely as the LORD your God lives," she replied, "I don't have any bread—only a handful of flour in a jar and a little olive oil in a jug. I am gathering a few sticks to take home and make a meal for myself and my son, that we may eat it—and die." Elijah said to her, "Don't be afraid. Go home and do as you have said. But first make a small loaf of bread for me from what you have and bring it to me, and then make something for yourself and your son. For this is what the LORD, the God of Israel, says: 'The jar of flour will not be used up and the jug of oil will not run dry until the day the LORD sends rain on the land.'" She went away and did as Elijah had told her. So there was food every day for Elijah and for the woman and her family. For the jar of flour was not used up and the jug of oil did not run dry, in keeping with the word of the LORD spoken by Elijah.

—1 Kings 17:8–16

That summer, Ian wanted to live with Bob. I was sad that we wouldn't be living in our new home together, especially since Ian would be going to university in the fall. However, I knew it was important to respect Ian's choice and his perseverance in trying to develop a closer relationship with his father. However, Ian and Bob didn't spend much time together when Ian was at his father's house, so Ian came home often.

During one of Ian's times at home, he, Leona, Syd, and I went camping at Miller Lake. Our campsite was like an encampment. We each had our own tent, including Syd, who was set up in the dining tent. It was a bit ridiculous, but we enjoyed our privacy. Lying in my tent at night, I could hear the distinctive call of the loons echoing over the water. The loon that Dad carved for me reminds me of special family times. Other members of my extended family were at a cottage nearby, and we enjoyed spending time with them, too.

One evening, several of us were at a campfire near the lake. The moon was reflecting in an awesome shimmering ribbon on the water. It was a very beautiful, peaceful scene that touched me deep inside. It was the first anniversary of my divorce being final. Now this date is also the anniversary of God's gift to me on that peaceful moonlit evening. God reminded me that He can wash over the dark and disturbing patterns of my tapestry with beauty and peace.

My grade-school friend Helen and I had connected occasionally after I moved to Strathroy but more frequently in the year since my separation. Helen and her husband were separated for a while too. However, when it became apparent that they were going to reconcile, we decided that we wouldn't visit with each other for a while so she could focus on her situation.

I didn't see Helen for a few months, but when I next visited her, it was obvious that something was terribly wrong. She was walking very awkwardly. Within days she was diagnosed with multiple sclerosis. After her diagnosis, I occasionally had an opportunity to help her a bit. I took her for a few acupuncture appointments, and I helped her sort through all her personal things and household items when her family moved.

My new house was within walking distance of Helen's new home. One day Helen and I went out for lunch to a place within walking distance of her home so she could use her scooter. Her disease progressed rapidly. She lost skills and mobility faster than she was able to adapt to the changes. It was difficult to witness her deterioration, but it was good to be pulled away from my own situation and to recognize that I was blessed to have the set of problems that I had. Helen maintained her strong faith in God, and through the years it was always a blessing to spend time with her.

———————

Ian was accepted into the co-op math program at the University of Waterloo, which involved a semester of school followed by a semester of work. He and I went to the bank to arrange for financial aid. Initially I was unable to help him get a loan because of my line of credit for the house. However, because I'd had a raise in the previous few months, we were able to get him a student line of credit. A few days later, I wrote, "Tonight I was figuring out finances—for paying residence and tuition—and I am once again amazed at how financially blessed I am. Working part-time is *the pits* sometimes, but it certainly pays well." On Sunday, September 3, Leona and I took Ian to Waterloo and helped him get a bit settled into his room in residence.

———————

When Ian was no longer lived at home, visits with Bob became more challenging. Ian and Leona had to be picked up from and returned to two different locations. One Saturday to Sunday visit was especially challenging. Ian called me late Sunday afternoon as Bob had no idea how he would get Ian and Leona back to their respective places of residence within the time frame he had allotted himself. After I had a heated debate with Bob on the phone, I realized that none of this was Ian's or Leona's fault. I agreed to drive to a meeting spot and then drive north to take Ian back to Waterloo before driving back south to Strathroy with Leona, about three hundred kilometres of driving.

I knew things weren't good when Ian didn't even say goodbye to his father. Both he and Leona were upset because Bob had dropped them off at his place on Saturday evening and then went out with his girlfriend for the evening. I wrote, "Why am I helping with driving if they aren't visiting with Bob anyway? I deplore the way Bob is treating the kids." There were so many emotions inside of me that I didn't know how to handle. Trusting God was my only option. After that, Ian and Leona only visited Bob if they were able to borrow my car so they could come and go as they pleased. I lived within walking distance of work and church, so there was seldom a problem.

———

I didn't have paid sick time, so it was challenging when I was ill for two weeks. The jar of oil didn't empty. A short time later, I had an accident with my car. The damage was mainly at the front, and I didn't think it was terribly serious. But, when my car was assessed, I was told it was a write-off. I begged the insurers to consider fixing my car, as my money from the house was still not available to me. My request was granted, and my car was returned to me two weeks later. Even though God was meeting my financial needs, I was unsettled about not having the money from the sale of the matrimonial home.

———

During the first fall living in my house, I had many days of feeling alone and uncertain. Ian was gone for school, and Leona was often in the quiet of her room. During my walk one cloudy morning, the sun suddenly and briefly peeked out at me. I felt like God was saying "good morning" to me. Seeing that glimpse of God in nature reminded me of His love for me, and I began noticing more than glimpses; I was seeing awesome displays! I had an east-west walk to and from work and saw many beautiful sunrises and sunsets. The neighbourhood was an amazing display of fall colours. My street was lined with maple trees on both sides, with myriad shades of yellow, gold, orange, and red. It was a great time for walking: to Dad and Mom's apartment, to work, with the dog. God's nearness and care felt abundantly clear as I saw Him through the beauty of nature.

———

Soon another blessing was added—more social interaction at work. I transferred to working part time on the medical unit where I had previously worked full time. Once again I was working with a larger team and had the opportunity to spend more time getting acquainted with patients and their families. I was disappointed when I found out that I didn't get the temporary full-time position I had applied for. Once again I had thought I had the most seniority of anyone who would apply for the position. I almost took it personally that nurses who knew that I was a struggling single mother applied for a position that I thought I desperately needed. I wrote, "I must have been counting on it more that I realized…I came up to cry on my bed and felt immediately surrounded by God's love. *He is in control!*"

———

Ian came home for Christmas break at the end of the first semester. One of his exams had been rescheduled due to a snowstorm, so he had to go back to Waterloo to write it. To make things less stressful, I offered to drive him the morning of his exam. Even though the weather was good and the roads were clear, we decided to leave really early. We would have breakfast in Waterloo so Ian could relax when we got there.

I'm not sure why we didn't travel our usual way. After an hour of our two-hour trip, the engine oil light came on, and I pulled into the nearest service station. A service man came out to assist us, and when he raised the hood, there was literally a fire burning there. The car was quickly pushed away from the gas pumps. Fortunately, the small fire was quickly extinguished.

I asked if there was a place where we could rent a car, as we needed to get to Waterloo urgently. There was a rental place two businesses further down the road, but they didn't open for an hour. It was 7:00 a.m.; the car rental place didn't open until 8:00 a.m., and Ian's exam started at 9:00 a.m. The business in between the service station and the car rental place was a restaurant. Ian and I went there for breakfast while we waited. Poor Ian— adrenalin was pumping through him so hard that his teeth were chattering. It was a very anxious time for him.

We went to the car rental place as soon as it opened. We explained our situation, and they said it would take us the whole hour we had to get to Waterloo. At first they were going to get us a car from behind the building, but then they decided that a warm car inside the garage would be better as it was ready to go. We left immediately. As Ian and I were driving down the road, I said to him, "I don't even know what colour this car is. I hope I can find it back after I park it." Praise the Lord, our drive was uneventful, and Ian arrived in his examination room *just in time.* It certainly wasn't the best conditions under which to write an exam, but he passed the course.

On our return to get our car, the first thing the car rental man did was ask Ian how the exam had been. The same thing happened at the service centre. I was touched that these men cared about Ian's exam, and Ian was too. The men at the service centre hadn't been able to find the oil leak. They sent us home with extra oil and instructions to check the oil every fifteen minutes. They only charged us for the cost of the oil. We had to add oil once on our way home, and by the time we arrived in Strathroy, the car was warm enough that the men at my usual service station were able to find the leak. I returned home with my car intact, and Ian and I still had the energy to celebrate our family Christmas by opening our gifts that evening.

I experienced so many emotions that day. I could see God throughout so much of what happened—the location of where our problem happened, the co-operation of everyone to try to get us to Waterloo, our arrival in Waterloo on time, the men asking Ian how his exam had been, our arrival home with the problem fixed. Could I doubt that there is a God who cares? I suppose I could ask why the leak had happened in the first place, but what I learned from the blessings far outweighed the challenges.

———

On Saturday, February 3, 2001, we celebrated Dad's eightieth birthday. My brother Len came from BC for the celebration and preached in our church the next day. Eight years later at Dad's funeral, Pastor Fred talked about that day. He said, "I was sitting in Westmount Christian Reformed Church, in a pew—my first Sunday there, their new minister—not on the pulpit. As the minister was preaching, I noticed a man, an older man, listening. His body bent towards the preacher; his head, motionless; mouth partly open. It was as if he was feasting on every word that the minister proclaimed. I marvelled, and I checked him out a couple times during the sermon. A few days later, after inquiry, I found out that the man was Mr. Batterink. And I found out that the minister was his son. And I thought, *No wonder he was listening so intently.* But I saw that look again, a few years later, when his grandson was preaching. But truthfully, Mr. Batterink loved to go into the house of the Lord and to gaze on the beauty of the Lord as expressed in the songs, the Scripture readings, confessions, and the proclamation of the Word." Dad's example was a blessing to his family.

———

In February 2001 I got news from my lawyer that things were developing with the financial settlement. This was great news. However, progress was very slow. Mid-May, my lawyer called. He told me that he had received notice from Bob's lawyer that there would be no need for child support, because the children were independent and self-supporting. My lawyer wondered when Ian and Leona had quit school. Nothing had changed. Ian was in his first year at university, and Leona was still in secondary school. It was like our lawyers weren't even looking at the same situation. I had hoped we would have a settlement soon. It was very difficult news to hear.

The time of waiting for the financial settlement was also difficult for some members of my extended family. They thought I should be pushing harder to get things resolved, that I was being too soft with Bob, and that my lawyer and I should fight harder for "justice." I remembered how blessed I had felt when my lawyer was recommended to me. I was pleased that we were doing everything possible so I wouldn't have to take Bob to court (1 Corinthians 6:1–7). Besides, going to court would cost a lot of money and cause more strife. Trusting God in this situation was a decision I had to make. I had seen examples of how well God could orchestrate His plans for my good.

———•———

I was wearing a winter coat that I really didn't like, but I was reluctant to spend money on something I didn't *need*. I sensed God saying to me, "Annette, how can I bless you if you won't let Me?" It gave me the courage to drive to the Sears outlet store to do some shopping. I found a coat I liked at a very reasonable sale price. This episode gave me the courage to once again spend my money a little more freely. We went out for supper rather than picking up fast food when I needed a break, and I began doing some minor house improvements. It was better to feel blessed by what I had than to always feel like I was scraping by.

———•———

When I had my yearly physical, my doctor told me that my emotional challenges weren't only from recent changes and the trauma of my divorce but also from the years of living in a stressful situation. I had to be more patient with myself. My doctor felt that more exercise would help me emotionally. So I tried running. One morning as I was running, a young boy waiting for his school bus said, "Look at that old lady trying to run!" I decided that walking would be a better option. I usually walked with Syd, and sometimes Shadow joined us. Our pets were great additions to our family. Syd loved each of us unconditionally, and Shadow spent many hours curled up with Leona when she had a headache.

In 2001, I became more technologically savvy. On March 13, 2001, I used Interac for the first time and, on April 9, 2001, I sent my first email.

Many times in the quiet of my room I poured out my heart to God and then wrote my thoughts in my journal. In the beginning of 2001, I was becoming weary and unsettled. I wrote, "In a few years it may be time to leave Strathroy." Without completion of my dealings with my lawyer, I felt stuck, waiting to step into my future. I wrote, "The past month has been one of realizing that *everything belongs to God*: the house, money, Ian, Leona, job search, Bob. We take ownership of way too many things." I realized that I was carrying burdens I wasn't meant to carry, but I wasn't sure how to move forward.

When Mom told me that some relatives were coming from the Netherlands for my parents' fifty-fifth anniversary in June, I wrote, "I dread the extra busyness." I wanted the house to look great inside and out. I created new flowerbeds, reseeded some of the lawn, painted the bathroom, and switched the ugly pink towel racks for white ones. My plans were ambitious, time-consuming, and probably not necessary. However, getting those jobs done gave me a sense of accomplishment and helped make the house "mine."

Thanks to extra driving by Clarence and Ed, Ian was able to join us for our summer family events even though he was doing a semester at university. We celebrated Dad and Mom's anniversary with an open house in June and a barbecue in Clarence's backyard later that summer, when Len and his family were in Ontario. In July, Ian, Leona, and I took Oma out for supper for her eightieth birthday. And when Leona, Syd, and I stayed at a camping cabin for a week, Ian joined us for the weekend. He enjoyed sitting around a campfire as much as I did, so it was great to have him there. I was thankful to have time to watch the fire, look at the stars in the sky, and just be still!

On September 11, 2001, Leona was home from school, as she wasn't feeling well. I had the TV on in the dining room. A news alert flashed across the screen: a plane had crashed into one of the twin towers of the World Trade Center in New York City. It seemed like an awful accident. I went downstairs to watch more news with Leona. Then a second plane hit the other tower, and it was obvious that something terrible was happening. It was one of the scariest days of my life.

The news kept getting worse and worse as both towers collapsed within two hours. A third plane crashed into the Pentagon, and a fourth plane crashed into a field near Shanksville, Pennsylvania, after its passengers tried to overcome the hijackers. The world felt out of control, and I wondered what would happen next. My thoughts soon turned to Ian. He was doing a co-op term in Ottawa, and I wondered if it was a bad time to be in the capital city of Canada. Would our country be attacked too? It was good to hear the sound of Ian's voice later that day. The world developed a "new normal" after that day. Our sense of security had been badly shaken.

By the end of my marriage I had been quite isolated from most people except the nurses I worked with. When I read about divorce recovery, I often read about the benefit of connecting with girlfriends. This was frustrating for me at first, but I was slowly connecting with people again. I continued to socialize with my Divorce Care friends. I enjoyed my time with family much more, as I was no longer doing a balancing act between Bob and them. And I was able to walk over to Dad and Mom's apartment to visit. The walk was especially lovely when crunching through the fall leaves. Working outdoors helped me feel better too. I enjoyed the exercise of raking leaves, and Mary's help and company were always appreciated.

The second year I lived in my house, I offered to have my extended family over on Christmas Day. The planning started early; I spent a day cooking and baking in preparation for our family Christmas and for us during the holidays. The house got a major cleaning. I wrote, "I've been through every closet and drawer once this year. I haven't been able to accomplish that in years." Living in a house that was a construction zone for ten years had been a challenge. It felt good to be an organized home-maker. The Christmas Day gathering went well. I enjoyed entertaining others in my home. I wrote, "Being on my own still doesn't feel 'right' but it no longer feels 'wrong'—I'm okay."

I was still occasionally having panic attacks. I had medication and was becoming better at preventing a full-blown episode from happening. For relaxation, I cross-stitched. I began the "tradition" of cross-stitch-ing a border on a bib for each of my great-nephews and great-nieces. I thought about the parents and child often as I stitched. I had no idea then how many of those little people would be born, but I can honestly say the number is greater than I had anticipated.

In 1998, when Bob and I separated, I had been working on a cross-stitch sampler with Psalm 23:6 on it: "Surely goodness and mercy shall follow me all the days of my life: and I will dwell in the house of the LORD forever" (KJV). During the first difficult months on my own, I found it very difficult to do any stitching. It didn't feel like "goodness and mercy" were a part of my life. I thought I would complete the proj-ect and give it away. But God was working in my heart and spirit as I stitched. Soon I was planning to hang it in my bedroom. Then, for my birthday in 2002, I got a gift card from Ed and Mary to have a cross-stitch project framed. I immediately knew that I would frame my Psalm 23:6 sampler. I hung it over the couch in my living room, and it's been hang-ing in a prominent place in my home for years.

———————

At the beginning of 2002, it had been almost two years since the mat-rimonial house had sold, and the money was still tied up at the lawyers. Bob had some lawyer changes that slowed the process. Interest rates were down, so I was a bit more secure financially. Then my lawyer called to tell me that we had an agreement that just needed to be finalized through the courts. However, soon after that Bob called to tell me he was having problems getting his file from his lawyer and needed money. I wrote, "It would almost be funny if it wasn't so frustrating." I called my lawyer and had him handle the situation. My waiting continued. There was too much frustration (and sometimes hurt) during this recovery stage of "exploring" for me to advance to the next stage. God's timing for me to "become" me would be perfect. Meanwhile, He continued to guide me forward slowly in various ways.

———

One night, I could see a scenario in my mind. I was being sheltered, safe and secure in a nest. Then it was like God was saying to me, "It's time to get out of the nest, Annette. It's time to fly!" It was good! It was what I needed. God had allowed me a time of looking inward, of recovering from pain and disappointment. However, it was time for things to change. My life needed to become less focused on dealing with emotional pain and more focused on living life.

This was followed by a season of God teaching me how to live in my "new normal." Some lessons are still being perfected in me. At some point, I heard a sermon by my brother Len about waiting. He said that it is sometimes too easy to *not* do anything effective while waiting. I needed to hear that. I also heard about "active waiting," that we should wait like we're in the starting blocks for a sprint, ready to go as soon as the gun fires.

There was an emotional release after I admitted to myself that I was angry at God. I had trusted for so long that God would heal my marriage, but He hadn't done that. Freedom from my marriage wasn't the solution I had been praying for, but I had to trust God and what He had allowed to happen in my life. God is God, and He loves me more than I could ever imagine. God loves me more than He loved my marriage.

Over time, I felt freedom from my marriage, but I still wasn't totally free. The institution of marriage and the marriage covenant were important enough to me that the enemy, the father of lies, knew he could rob me of my joy again and again by pouring guilt and shame over me. I wasn't even really sure what I felt guilty about or what I was ashamed of. These feelings kept me from moving forward in freedom.

I was blessed one Sunday when Pastor Fred preached about Peter and Cornelius. I was reminded that God said, "Do not call anything impure that God has made clean" (Mark 10:15). God so lovingly and graciously kept showing me how much He loved me. Sometimes He whispered to my heart the words of Jeremiah 31:3: "I have loved you with an everlasting love." However, the enemy continued at times to rob me of my joy with guilt and shame. God was infinitely patient with me.

One evening I read a story about a woman who had been abused by her mother. She saw a vision of her mother the way God had created her mother to be, not the way her mother had become after the difficulties of her life. I began to pray that I might be able to see Bob as he had been created to be. It hasn't always been possible, and I fall short so often, but trying has been worthwhile. The enemy was the devil, not Bob.

Shortly after the end of our marriage, Bob had wanted me to read a book about co-dependency. I gave it back to him after reading a few pages. At the time the focus would have been on trying to fix our marriage, but now I could focus on trying to fix me. I readily accepted when a co-worker offered me the loan of *Co-Dependent No More* by Melody Beattie. The book helped me put a label on the insights I had already gained from doing the twelve-step program.

When Mom and Dad moved to Strathroy, they had looked forward to helping me now that I was on my own again. However, Dad soon started having more health problems, but they could help financially. They gave me some money to have some indoor painting done. I hired a friend to do the painting for me. He had also been recently divorced, and I noticed that our conversations were all about him. He never once asked how I was doing. It wasn't a bad thing necessarily, but I was glad that I noticed. I had gained some insights from what I had read.

One night, I had a dream in which I remembered those "alone—waiting" times of my childhood. Alone with my siblings in the car waiting for my mother to come out of the hospital; alone on the couch when I had rheumatic fever; alone while the new baby chicks were getting older by the minute. I realized that there was no fear, frustration, or anger attached to those memories. I had felt safe and knew I had to wait. God in His providence had taught me some valuable lessons about being alone and waiting when I was a child. In the days and years following the end of my marriage, I needed to use what I had learned. There were a lot of alone times—alone at the end of the day with my thoughts and feelings that no one could understand; alone as a parent to my children. There was lots of waiting: waiting for the house to sell, waiting for the lawyers to be done their work, waiting for the pain to ease, and waiting as again and again I sorted out my feelings about remarriage. I needed to remember to "be joyful in hope, patient in affliction, faithful in prayer" (Romans 12:12).

———————

During Leona's last year of high school. I wrote, "I have been feeling anxious lately—the idea of being *alone* next year is *awful*. I'm really starting to be bothered by that and must let it go. I have to be careful not to pick up 'any old man' just so I won't be alone. I think about remarriage a lot but realize more and more that Ian and Leona need a period of stability." I also wrote, "God, it is my desire to have an earthly husband again someday. I want it to be someone who will be a good spouse, and if/when I'm remarried, I hope Ian and Leona gain a wonderful friend. Please take this desire away if it's not Your will. Meanwhile, help me live for You." With this kind of "exploring," I was starting to become unstuck.

———————

Leona's life was different than I ever dreamed it would be. She still had headaches all the time and missed many social activities. I was hurt when people thought that she could do something to change her situation. She became more independent all the time and certainly felt like her life had some quality. In the spring, she qualified to run at OFSSA (Ontario Federation of Secondary School Athletic Associations) in the 3,000 metre run! She also attended her grade 12 prom.

It was an emotional experience for both of us when Leona received the E. C. McTavish award representing the high school she attended. The award recognized outstanding graduating students in the area's secondary schools who faced obstacles in their path and overcame these challenges. Her certificate said, "This kind, compassionate and intelligent student has succeeded in making a significant contribution within her school and community despite a recurring, debilitating affliction." I was finally able to silence some of those voices who had tried to question Leona's situation. Leona was rewarded for her perseverance and hard work at school and in athletics. In the photo taken for the award, Leona is framing her face with her running cleats.

———

In the spring of 2002, my parents bought a new car. A few weeks later I drove it to my nephew Ryan's wedding, as Dad and Mom seldom drove out of town or at night. They told me that their new car would be mine when they could no longer drive it. I had no idea when that day would be and hoped they would have some independence for a long time yet. I had borrowed Ed and Mary's van a few times but now decided to replaced my car with a van for ease in getting Ian and Leona's "stuff" to and from wherever they were living while in school. At the same auto place where I had purchased my last car, I found a dark green Venture van. When I went to pick the van up, it cost one dollar more than I was originally told, so Ian paid the difference.

When I had initially looked at the van, the very back seat was missing. I wasn't interested in buying a van with seating for only four people, as I often gave people rides. The salesman assured me that they would be on the lookout for another rear seat. Days later, there was a fatal accident with a Venture van in which a young boy was killed. Soon after, I got a call that a rear seat had been located. I wondered if it was from the accident, but I didn't really want to know. When Ian, Leona, and I took the van to show my parents, my mother noticed some glass under the rear seat. I was thankful for having a vehicle I could afford (with some help from my parents), but I needed to trust God with the way in which He had provided.

As I continued to explore life in my new reality, I started doing some activities that were a bit out of my comfort zone. When Ian gave me a gift certificate to the Grand Theatre for Mother's Day, I decided it would be the least stressful to attend a matinee. I don't remember the name of the play I saw, but I do remember something even better. I had been looking forward to going to the theatre but wasn't sure about going alone. When I got out of my car at a nearby parking lot, I heard a busker playing *Great Is Thy Faithfulness* on a trumpet. I knew the words of all the verses. "Strength for today and bright hope for tomorrow; Blessings all mine with ten thousand beside" are words from verse 3. I was overwhelmed by God's love for me. The timing was amazing, and this was the only hymn I heard the trumpeter play that day. This is a brilliant thread in my tapestry.

Later that summer, I rented a cottage at Port Franks on Lake Huron. Ian and Leona came during the day a few times, my parents came for an overnight visit, and one day I had a barbeque for ten family members. The evening after the barbeque, Dad, Mom, Ed, Mary, and I watched a Lake Huron sunset together. It was a beautiful, peaceful time to share as the sky turned orange and the glow of the sun slowly faded. During that week, it was good for me to spend time alone in that place. There can be such joy in the "simple" things of life.

Finally, the financial agreement papers were signed on July 26, 2002, almost two and a half years after we sold our house. I wrote, "I'll get just over half the amount of money I had originally hoped I'd get—I'll never be rich, but I am very blessed! I am able to get Ian and Leona their needs and some of their wants, too." Ironically, Bob and I had initially agreed that Ian, Leona, and I would be able to stay in the house until Leona finished high school. Then Bob changed his mind because he wanted the money *now,* which started the adventure we had been on. These years later, Leona had just completed high school. I tried not to gloat over that fact, but it did make me shake my head and smile. God's ways are mysterious!

Eventually I was able to remortgage the house and get rid of my line of credit. Bob had not paid child support during the negotiation phase, but now he started to pay some money directly to Ian and Leona. I had thought that life would feel much better once the settlement was done, but it wasn't a magic event. Ian, Leona, and I still had achiness, head-aches, and general malaise too often. We sometimes struggled to main-tain a healthy lifestyle. It was good that we continued to work through our feelings. I had long conversations with them, and their honesty hurt sometimes. Sometimes I hurt for them; sometimes I hurt for me.

———

Leona was briefly enrolled in a program at the University of Windsor in the fall of 2002. At first when Leona was gone, Syd was despondent. Leona had lain on him or beside him so often when she wasn't feeling well, and now, where was she? How could he take care of her? He lay on the floor outside her door for three days before he accepted that she wasn't coming out of her room any time soon. After Leona's orientation to her classes, I wrote, "Leona is not convinced she'll get the education she wants in the program she's in." Not investing time and money into something she didn't want seemed the best thing to do. After returning home, Leona often didn't feel well, and she was unable to find a job. It was a challenging season in her life and mine, as I tried to support her. The next year, Leona was accepted into the fitness and health promotion program at Humber College in Toronto.

At school, Ian found it difficult to keep up his class work and do everything he needed to do to find a job for the next semester. When he had applied for the co-op program he hadn't realized how time-con-suming searching for a job would be. Moving every four months was challenging and unsettling, too. He decided to transfer to the regular program, and he shared an apartment with his cousin Jon for the next two semesters. A *big* benefit of being in the regular program was that he was able to get much more involved with the cross-country team. When I was able, I enjoyed being a spectator on a crisp, cool fall afternoon and benefited from the time outdoors in nature.

One very memorable time in my nursing career was during the SARS (severe acute respiratory syndrome) epidemic. Between February and September 2003 Health Canada reported 438 probable or suspect cases of SARS, resulting in forty-three deaths, primarily in the Greater Toronto Area. It was a stressful time for nurses. Our hospital in Strathroy created two negative-pressure rooms. They had touchless flushing for the toilets and sensors for the taps to flow. These were quite new concepts at the time. We had no patients with SARS, so we used the rooms for other patients.

One day the room was occupied by a woman who was confused and had been disruptive. She needed assistance going to the bathroom, so I accompanied her. It shocked and upset her when the toilet flushed as soon as she stood up. It only got worse when she reacted by leaning over the sink and the water started flowing. I felt sorry for her, but I could hardly keep from laughing. It was funny!

In April of 2003, I attended the fiftieth anniversary of Forest Christian Reformed Church with my parents, Mary and Ed. It was good to see familiar faces from long ago, but it was a bit difficult to share some of my story. "Divorced" was still a difficult word for me. A few weeks after the church anniversary, I attended Clarence and Jeri's twenty-fifth anniversary party. It was a painful reminder that I wouldn't be celebrating my own twenty-fifth wedding anniversary in two years. As I write this, I'm not having much patience with myself and some of the struggles I had. I am becoming more aware of how hard it must be for others to watch a family member struggle through their loss and pain.

Later that summer, Ian, Leona, and I took a few days for the long drive to Kenora, Ontario, when Mary's son Jon got married. We stopped briefly to visit with my friend Margo in Thunder Bay. When we arrived in Kenora, Jon was pacing about, waiting for family to arrive. My van arrived first from eastern Ontario, then within minutes his brother Ryan drove in from Michigan, and before we went inside, his other siblings arrived from Winnipeg. It was only because of an accident along the way that Ian, Leona, and I arrived when we did. It was fun to watch Jon welcome us all, amazed at the timing.

Our wedding hosts had events planned from Thursday evening to Sunday evening for Jon's "far-away relatives." We were fed several times and given free accommodations. Several of our activities were on or near Lake of the Woods: a barbeque on an island, boating to a lunch engagement, watching the wedding party arrive at the reception in boats, and a day at the father of the bride's cottage. Our warm welcome, added to the beauty of nature all around us, made our trip a great mini-vacation.

The evening of the wedding there were fireworks, but God was not to be outdone. He finished the evening with a display of northern lights. After the wedding I wrote, "I danced like I've never danced before at the reception—so much fun!" My nephew Tim and his wife, Leanne, joined us on the drive home. With two teams, one person to drive and one to watch for wildlife, we were able to complete the trip home without stopping except for food and gas and bathroom breaks. I was hopeful for better days ahead and more new beginnings.

It was the beginning of better days when I got a reduced-full-time position. Mary and Ed celebrated with me by sending me flowers. I had been working part-time since before the end of my marriage. For six years I had tried to pick up as many hours as I could, whenever I could. One year I only had nine full weekends off, and the next year I had eleven full weekends off. It was still uncomfortable for me to go to church alone, so working those weekends may have been a blessing for me. However, my absences must have made life feel more difficult for Ian and Leona.

Now, my life started having a more consistent routine, and I finally had vacation and sick time again. The schedule wasn't ideal, as I always worked nights before a weekend off, but it was an improvement. I no longer got my "in lieu of benefits" paid out, so my paycheque was smaller. But now the financial settlement after the divorce was complete, and a smaller paycheque was no problem. It had been hard to see the possibility of blessings during the "storm," but God's timing was right!

———

The days of "exploring" after my divorce had many challenges. I didn't make much progress emotionally during the years that Bob's belongings were still in the home or while I was waiting for the financial settlement to be completed. When I was having a pity party, I said negative things that I wasn't proud of. Many people told me that I now seemed more relaxed and happier, and that was good to hear. With God's help and guidance, I was becoming unstuck from the past. God provided for, loved, protected, and embraced me, and He opened my eyes to His powerful presence in my situations. God was leading me into a better way of living.

chapter twelve

ON MY OWN AGAIN—BECOMING ME

*Then they cried to the LORD in their trouble, and he saved them from
their distress. He brought them out of darkness, the utter darkness, and
broke away their chains.*

—Psalm 107:13–14

AT THE BEGINNING OF AUGUST 2003, I AGAIN ANSWERED A PERSONAL AD IN A
church-related magazine. In the ad, the man asked for a woman yearn-
ing for wholeness, and I wanted to know what he meant. After I got
Jurgen's well-written email response, I was looking forward to sharing
ideas about personal growth. I hadn't necessarily been looking to start
connecting with someone, but I *had* responded to a personal ad. Soon,
Ian was back at Waterloo, and Leona had started her course at Humber
College in Toronto. My nest was empty except for the pets, Syd and
Shadow, and the emails helped me in the adjustment.

Jurgen lived many miles away. After three months of corresponding, he had a business meeting in a nearby city that might give us an opportunity to meet each other. I was disappointed that plans didn't work
out for the evening we thought we would meet. However, God had other plans for me for that evening. Shortly before supper, a young woman
I knew from church called to ask me if I'd like to go to see *The King and
I* at the Stratford Shakespearean Theatre that very evening. The friend
she had planned to attend with was ill. It was an hour drive to Stratford,
so I didn't have much time to get ready, but—wow! It was an awesome
opportunity, and the play was amazing.

I wanted to trust God no matter how things worked out with Jurgen. I met him a few days after going to the theatre and again shortly
after Christmas when he was visiting family near Toronto. We had fun

together—long drives, lots of walking, and some great conversations. Soon we were talking on the phone once a week. However, I was becoming confused about Jurgen's intentions. Hadn't he been the one to put the ad in the paper? My brother Len told me to ask myself some questions: Does he want a relationship? Does he want a relationship with me? I was scared to know the answers.

While contemplating the possibility of a future with Jurgen, I wrote, "I can't imagine how we would work together for the Lord." Jurgen was quite involved with his church in a good and positive way, but it wasn't something that I could imagine myself doing. I hoped that if I got married again, there would be a partnership in serving the Lord together. I'm not sure if God placed this idea on my heart, but it became increasingly important to me as an issue that would need to be addressed.

We connected for eight months. Then Jurgen told me that he enjoyed our times together but had never anticipated the possibility of a long-distance relationship when he had placed his ad. He had hoped for and still preferred to find someone he could have one-on-one connections with on a regular basis. A long-distance relationship would have required a great effort from both of us. I was hurt and disappointed for a while. Eventually, I was proud of myself. I had been able to sort through the maze of a relationship and accept the end when it came. The decision that Jurgen and I made to move forward on our own rather than maintaining a friendship helped me to turn from looking back. I began to look forward. I was thankful for that little push into my future.

———

Then I *finally* got a permanent full-time position and a much better schedule. Once a month I had an extended weekend off, from 7:00 p.m. on Thursday until 7:00 p.m. on Monday. I gave a big, deep sigh of relief. I hadn't had a full-time job since April of 1996. God had graciously supported me and my family financially, but it had not been easy. Many days I had been very tired and had little energy to care for myself or to be the parent I wished I could be. God's ways are not always easy to understand.

I had to trust my tapestry designer. I could only see the underside of the masterpiece God was creating.

———

In my empty nest with only the pets at home, I adjusted to the new routine of life. I was the only person available to walk Syd. When it was raining hard, Syd and I had the outside world to ourselves. I found it cozy somehow to be under my umbrella, surrounded by all the many raindrops, with my faithful friend right beside me. In the fall, when the apples were plentiful, Mary and I had "Apple Day" with Dad and Mom in Mary's kitchen. Together we made applesauce and sliced apples for the freezer. There was lots of fun and laughter during these times together.

———

In the evenings, Ian, Leona, and I sometimes connected on MSN Messenger. We were able to have a three-way conversation and share what we were doing. Often the best times for me were when Ian and Leona started typing back and forth to each other and I sat back and watched the conversation unfold. Ian was running on the cross-country team and was enjoying it. Leona felt she was dealing with her headaches better, and she was finding opportunities for running too. Together we arranged plans for weekend visits home.

———

I celebrated my fiftieth birthday on February 14, 2004. The surprises started early in the day. A florist delivered a mug filled with flowers from my co-workers that said "Simply Fantastic at 50." My birthday celebrations were simply fantastic. Dad took all of us out for a surprise birthday supper that evening. My parents, my children, my siblings, several nieces and nephews, and those added to the family over the years were there. My brother Len, who lived in BC, had timed a visit with Dad and Mom so he could be there too.

The next morning an announcement was made in church that the Batterink clan was in town for a birthday. After the service, I got many hugs and congratulations from my church family. I had felt sad that I would not have a twenty-fifth wedding anniversary. I told my family the birthday celebration was an awesome replacement. My life had been celebrated.

A few days later, I wrote, "The excitement about my birthday has passed; now I'm just a fifty-year-old lady. I certainly don't *feel* that old. I'm thankful for the zest and enjoyment in life that I still experience. Hopefully I will do so for many years." This statement was a huge contrast from how I felt at the end of my marriage when I was not able to go for long walks and had little enjoyment in life. Thank You, God, my healer!

One Friday evening soon after, I wrote, "I become more and more certain about leaving Strathroy—probably not until Ian and Leona are finished school." Two days later, Pastor Fred preached on Abraham picking up his tent. "The LORD had said to Abram [later Abraham], 'Go from your country, your people and your father's household to the land I will show you'"(Genesis 12:1). But for now, it was good that Ian, Leona, and I lived down the street and around the corner from Dad and Mom. It was a blessing to live so close to my parents and to have Ian and Leona spend time with them, just talking about life one-to-one or two-to-one.

Sometimes Mom had Ian and Leona in for meals when I was working, pancakes for lunch on a Saturday or a hot meal after church on Sunday. They would loop past my parents' apartment when they were running, and if they were gone for a long time, I guessed that they were visiting with my parents out on their patio. It became an annual event for Ian, Leona, and I to have dinner at their apartment on New Year's Day. It was Mom's chance to do something special during the holiday season. My favourite memories of Dad are when he or I would say something silly and we would give each other "the look."

On one afternoon visit, I talked to Dad about how frustrating I found it that I wasn't able to be more involved at church because of my shift work. At one time I had been asked to be a table leader for Alpha, a course that explores the basics of the Christian faith. Later I was asked if I would consider being a pastoral elder. It bothered me that I wasn't able to do these things. For years, my job and my "other life" were quite separate in my mind. Dad said he felt that nursing was my calling and that I was doing what I was meant to do in my role there. There is only one life to live: day by day, step by step, with Father God.

———

As I became more practised at "becoming me," Ian and Leona continued to struggle. Some of the summers when they were home from school they had jobs, and some summers they didn't. Leona still had headaches, and it was a difficult balancing act for me between giving Ian a nudge and trusting his own decisions. I was pleased that he continued with his education and his running. I wrote, "Ian and Leona being at home every day is difficult. I pray that God may strengthen and guide me in this situation." I tried to be patient with them as they sorted through their hurts and frequently felt physically ill.

In the past, Ian and Leona had *survived* while I focused on trying to make the marriage survive. It was difficult for me to accept and admit that I didn't always give my children the support they needed. There were too many times when my inaction spoke more loudly than my actions ever would have. It was painful when Ian told me that he remembered me as a mother who worked and slept and that he sometimes felt like he had no parents. Leona, especially, needed me to admit that my lack of responsiveness to their needs had added to their painful experiences.

Some years later, Leona told me that she had felt like life wasn't worth living if her life was going to be like mine. She had been eleven years old when she first felt that way. She told me her freedom started when she saw me "break free." She could then explore possibilities too. God knew the end from the beginning and He knew what had been happening in my daughter's heart when I didn't. God knew how necessary change was for all of us.

One evening I read Proverbs 14:26: "Whoever fears the LORD has a secure fortress, and for their children it will be a refuge." I wrote, "When I trust God, it brings security to Ian and Leona. The shelter of the confidence of His care is a wonderful place to be." Later I added, "In many ways, I think Ian would feel more secure if I felt more secure." I wondered how my children's lives might have been different if I had been different. I had to learn to accept what God allowed to happen in our lives and to remember that God loved Ian and Leona more than I ever could. For too long I had carried burdens I wasn't meant to carry and tried to solve problems I was never going to be able to solve. God wanted me to be victorious over my situations, not burdened by them.

———

I decided to go camping at Miller Lake, but Ian and Leona chose to stay at home. Ed, Mary, their daughter, and her family were at a cottage there. I enjoyed camping by myself. One very peaceful morning I was up before six o'clock. I walked to the lake and sat on a bench. There was a mist over the water, and ducks were quietly swimming about. It seemed like they didn't want to disturb the silence either. I wrote, "Do I trust God? Does He have to supply things *my* way to satisfy me? Or can I live each day knowing that *each day matters*? God has been so patient with me about this." The ducks and I had been quiet for quite a while when someone made a loud noise opening a door and then began to noisily sweep the porch of their cottage. A new day had begun.

———

That fall, things were different for our family, in a good way. I was working every other weekend, so there were fewer opportunities for Ian and Leona to come home. They were both involved in things at school, so it all evolved as it should have. A mission team from our church was going to Honduras in February 2005, and I signed up to be part of Team Honduras. Planning meetings and fundraising for Team Honduras were ongoing. It was good for me to be involved with something besides work and home. Financially, becoming part of the team had not been an easy decision. I had to trust that God would provide the funds I needed.

During the months before our departure, I spent time on Christian singles sites, especially Christian Café. I wrote, "Will I ever get married again? Only if I fall in love, I hope!" I found it helpful to read the profiles and find out what people's expectations were. Some of the men seemed like good people; some seemed like more of what I had already experienced in my marriage. How was God going to direct this situation? I needed to "wait for the LORD; be strong and take heart and wait for the LORD" (Psalm 27:14). I became pen pals with Ron, a nurse from California, who had been on several mission trips. His accounts of his experiences were good to read before I went to Honduras.

———

At Humber College, Leona was doing well, and running was an important part of her well-being. Leona joined Campus Christian Fellowship with a classmate, Linda. It was a busy time at school as they also needed to find job placements. One day Leona had an interview in downtown Toronto. To try to limit the amount of stress Leona had and thereby decrease the likelihood of her having a headache, I planned to drive her to the interview.

When we were ready to leave the college, the van wouldn't start. My very organized daughter had already investigated the transit system in case I wasn't able to come, so we took the bus and subway. We still arrived for the interview on time. It was an adventure Leona was prepared for. I was very proud of how she handled the whole situation.

The next day, I called CAA (the Canadian Automobile Association) to see about getting my van towed for repairs. When the tow truck driver arrived, he said, "I hope you want to get towed home." He wanted to get out of the city for a while. When I asked him how much it would cost, he said forty dollars. Perfect! The driver and I enjoyed seeing the fall colours between Toronto and Strathroy. It was good to have the van back home, and I didn't even have to do the driving!

Ian was running with the University of Waterloo cross-country team and at the end of the season was named most improved cross-country runner. In mid-November, Ian and the team ran at the Canadian Inter-university Cross-Country Championships in Guelph, Ontario. It was exciting to see student runners from twenty universities across Canada, and I was proud that Ian was part of the event.

My brother Clarence had told me he might attend, so I was watching out for him. I watched one particular man walking towards me. Sunglasses and a baseball cap made recognition difficult. It was a cool day, so I was wearing a coat with the hood pulled tightly around my head. The man totally ignored me. So just before he passed me, I dared say, "Clarence?" I thought that might catch his attention. It was my brother. We were surprised we had so much difficulty spotting each other. It was great that Clarence came, and I know that Ian appreciated it.

When Ian and Leona were home for Christmas we played some board games, and Ian said I was too uncompetitive to be fun to play with. It was something I hadn't recognized in myself before but definitely wanted to be more aware of. I was touched when Ian gave me a cross-stitch project with the saying "Dare to Dream." It made me even more aware that Ian and Leona needed to see *me* move forward with my life, too.

I learned that day-to-day living was the easier part. It was the once-a-year events like Christmas that still didn't feel "normal." That Christmas had an additional challenge. Ian and Leona noticed how much Syd was aging. He had not been running with Ian and Leona for a while and now was sometimes uninterested in walking too. However, when we opened our gifts, he was once again "our big kid." It was fun watching him. He seemed to enjoy our excitement. He was definitely happiest when we were all together, preferably in the same room.

As I prepared for my time in Honduras, God was faithful! The donations for me as an individual were beyond amazing. I got donations from friends and family, including $1,000 anonymously donated to my Honduras account. I had enough money for everything I could think of, including kennel fees for Syd for fifteen days and spending money while I was in Honduras. Someone at work donated her steel-toed boots to me, which fit perfectly.

Before I left, I got an early birthday present from Ed and Mary. The previous fall, Mary and I had seen a "dog-warmer" in one of the shops we visited. It was a stuffed puppy with a removable rice-filled tummy that could be warmed up in the microwave. "Wow," I said to Mary, "that would be better than a man!" Ed and Mary gave me a dog-warmer for my birthday. It is a bubble of delight on my tapestry.

Shortly after midnight on February 11, Team Honduras departed from Strathroy for our flight to Honduras via Houston, Texas. Landing in Tegucigalpa, Honduras, was an experience. The airport had a very short (6,132 foot) runway. Due to the surrounding mountains, the approach resembled a zigzag. To line up with the runway, planes had to make a last-second 45-degree turn. Turn, drop, and stop. Everyone in the plane clapped when we had landed safely.

We were working on a HANDS project (Help Another Nation Develop Schools) through an organization that is now called EduDeo Ministries. El Verbo Christian School was located in Nueva Suyapa, part of the capital city of Tegucigalpa. Nueva Suyapa was a slum, considered by most to be the worst in Central America. The area had about two thousand residents until after Hurricane Fifi in 1974, when the government allowed people who were displaced by the hurricane to build there. The population quickly grew to thirty thousand, with little infrastructure to support the residents. It was in the midst of that crisis that the school was started.

During our time at the two campuses of El Verbo School, we made some cinder block walls and did some painting. Each team member seemed to find their own place where they contributed to what needed to be done. I carried more cinder blocks than I could count from point A to B to C until the blocks were where they were needed. We sifted lots of sand and mixed our own cement in a wheelbarrow, then moved the cement in pails to where it was needed. It's awesome to know that threads of my tapestry are part of this project.

Some scents trigger headaches for me, and I mentioned that in an email to my pen pal, Ron. He prayed that I wouldn't have a problem while I was in Honduras. Those prayers were answered. Even though the paint we used was thinned with a lot of paint thinner, and even though they melted plastic pop bottles in their burn barrel, I did not get a headache. We did ask them to move the burn barrel though, as the fumes were unhealthy for anyone to breathe.

We were often reminded that we were working in a tough neighbourhood. One of the schools had a gym behind it. It had been necessary to build a tunnel to join the gym to the school because of the interference of gangs with the school children. When soft drinks were delivered to the school, an armed guard was present. We never walked in the neighbourhoods without someone with us who was familiar to the people who lived there. A nuisance when walking was that most of the manhole covers had been stolen.

The school where we were working was high in the hills. Many of the families lived in homes that were only slightly larger than the shed in my backyard at home. Surrounded by the poverty of the neighbourhood where we were working, I could look down on the city of Tegucigalpa and the airport. One day I was overwhelmed by the knowledge that these people, who lived so differently than I did, experienced God's love in as real a way as I did. God met their needs just as He met mine. On the surface, our needs seemed so different, but we shared God's love and the blessing of being a part of His family. It was an amazing, blessed, humbling thing to experience the happiness of the Christians we met. They had so little, but it was enough!

My memories include the overwhelming poverty, the dust, the smoky atmosphere, the constant activity, the poor driving practices, toilets that didn't flush (we had to fill the tank with a pail of water), drinking bottled water, and most of our team members getting sick. Our Honduran construction leader sometimes spoke to me because I had learned just enough Spanish for him to consider me "the translator." I also remember how the steel shank went flying out of one of Ian's boots that a team member had borrowed. It happened when we were on our way off of the worksite for the last time on the last day. God's amazing timing!

Before I left for Honduras, Ian borrowed my van so he and Leona could attend the Team Honduras commissioning service and then come home again as soon as I returned. As I reflected on my own, I wondered how God would use my Honduras experience in "my world." He hadn't placed me in Honduras; my life was in Canada. My father often said that the more we have, the more we have to worry about. I became more conscious of that. It is a challenge to live in a culture that has so much and thinks we need more.

Syd's health had continued to decline. He was waking me up during the night, or during the day, as he was losing bowel control. If I worked a twelve-hour shift, Syd had accidents in the laundry room. I quietly cleaned up the mess on the laundry room floor before I fed him. It must have been hard for him, too. I was glad that the laundry room had always been "Syd's spot" when he was home alone. He felt safe and secure there, and it worked well having him there in the present situation. How much longer would Syd be with us?

My parents were aging too. They had always led active lives involving lots of people. Mobility was becoming a greater issue for Dad, and my mother missed being out and about with him. Sometimes Mom walked from their apartment to my home or phoned me to talk about Dad. She was hoping that the nurse in the family would know a solution to the problem. At one point I wrote, "Worrying about my parents seems overwhelming." Dad was a bit stubborn about using a walking aid, but he enjoyed the extra mobility he had when he started using a walker. He coped with his declining health quite well, but Mom found it increasingly difficult.

Whenever Ian or Leona left town for a while, Dad and Mom came to our house to say goodbye. Syd was not allowed in the living room, so Dad would sit on the edge of the couch nearest the dining room. Syd would edge close enough so Dad could reach him and give him some loving attention. The less mobile Dad became, the less attention I paid to how far Syd ventured into the living room. Dad and Syd were both aging, and watching the changes was difficult. My parents' role in my life was changing, as was my role in theirs. I was their chauffeur more often, and I began cutting Dad's hair. I was blessed to still feel their love and support for me and my family.

———

By the summer of 2005, Ian and Leona had completed their programs, Leona in fitness and health promotion at Humber College and Ian in math at the University of Waterloo. Both of them needed to make plans for their future. Leona's friend Linda from Humber had moved to Calgary, and Leona sent resumés there. I wrote, "Still no jobs—it bothers me a bit sometimes." I recognized that what everyone else could be thinking bothered me more than the fact that they weren't working. The weather that summer was often hot and humid. It made everyone tired, and we all had headaches more frequently.

One evening I read Luke 3:21–22: "When all the people were being baptized, Jesus was baptized too...And a voice came from heaven: 'You are my Son, whom I love; with you I am well pleased.'" I wrote, "What an awesome example of what a father-son (parent-child) relationship should be like." Did I tell my children that I was proud of them? Did they sense that I was proud of them? Shortly after, Ian read in a book about having an absentee father who is physically present. A father, though physically present, can, for various reasons, be unavailable to the child and his or her needs. These words were significant enough to Ian for him to share them with me. I knew that these comments could apply to a mother, too. Ian and Leona experienced my absence when I set poor boundaries and priorities. I couldn't undo the past, but I could try to change the present and the future.

It was, and continues to be, a huge blessing to me that, in spite of the lack of support they felt from their parents, Ian and Leona are able to feel the love of their heavenly Father. The blessings I received as Dad's daughter were being passed down to my children. I was thankful for the influence of their grandfather, my father. God is good and faithful through the generations!

———

By mid-summer, Leona and I felt that it was time to euthanize Syd, but Ian wasn't ready. Syd had a poor appetite and very poor bowel control, and his hearing and vision seemed to be affected too. Ian felt that Syd's quality of life came from being with us, and Syd still enjoyed being with us. On July 30, we all went for a walk, but not too far, as Syd wasn't able to do that. Five days later, Syd was outside with Ian in the evening when it started raining and thundering. Syd hated thunderstorms, but that evening he seemed unable to make himself climb the few steps into the house. He did eventually get inside, but Ian knew then that Syd's suffering was too much.

We were blessed to have a veterinarian in the family. When I called, Ed came to our home. He first gave Syd medication to make him comfortable. He left for a while, and we all spent time with Syd and said our goodbyes. Then Ed came back and gave the final medication. I had Syd cremated so we would have his ashes. He lived from February 2, 1994, to August 5, 2005. We missed him terribly!

Syd had been a best friend when the entire world felt crazy around us. He had been despondent when Leona went to Windsor, and he was worried about her. When I returned home from taking Ian to one of his co-op job placements, Syd came to the door, checked me out, looked past me for Ian, and figured it out. He just turned around and walked downstairs. Syd loved my boy too!

Through the seven years of adjustment after the divorce, we felt Syd's unconditional love for each of us. There had been many walks and runs, alone or together, in the day or in the evening. There had also been quiet times when Ian or Leona hugged and held Syd as they dealt with whatever emotion they were feeling. He truly had been God's gift to us!

Ian decided to take a program at Seneca College in Toronto, so he was back to school in the fall. At home, Leona acted as my personal trainer. It was good to work at taking care of my body with expert help. I was working physically at my job, caring for patients at the hospital, but there were imbalances in my muscle strength, and I had issues with my balance. It felt good and right to be focusing on myself more.

My Divorce Care friends and I tried to meet monthly, and through the years several other women joined us. While all the members were single, we called ourselves the UFOs—Unattached Singles Only. Eventually someone got married, and then already married women joined us, so we changed our name to the YaYas. When I put out an invitation for a UFO group at my church, I was surprised that it was mostly older widowed women who came. Several of them were Mom's friends. One gathering I especially remember is the evening we discussed whether we slept with our bedroom door open or closed. The smiles seemed especially big as they realized that the other women present knew exactly how they felt. It was refreshing. I was reminded of my Divorce Care experience and that Jesus had an inner circle of twelve select men too. There is power and connection in support groups, even those created for fun!

I started taking advantage of my days off and my paid vacation time. In the summer, with some family members, I experienced going close to Niagara Falls on a boat called *The Maid of the Mist*. It was an amazing experience to be surrounded by the power of nature, a wall of water in front of us and on two sides. I felt small and humbled yet safe and secure in the circumstances. In September, Ian, Leona, and I celebrated Mary's birthday on Toronto Island and went sailing with her son, Tim. This was followed by a road trip with Mary around Lake Superior. We visited our friend Margo near Thunder Bay and also stopped at the Terry Fox Memorial. There was a lot of beautiful, rugged scenery around the lake.

There was more! In November, Leona went to Cornwall for a job interview. We planned to go to Ottawa on Remembrance Day but decided to drive to Montreal on the afternoon of the tenth so we could say we had been in three of Canada's largest cities in three days: Toronto, Montreal, and Ottawa. Driving in Montreal was an adventure as we got a bit lost. We had planned to go to a mall but ended up going much farther into the city. I was proud of myself because, even in busy traffic, I didn't get honked at once. It was a shiny thread in my tapestry and great to be doing something just because it would be fun.

Standing close to the War Memorial in Ottawa on Remembrance Day was a great experience. It was a crisp, clear, cold morning, but the crowd was large, and I think that helped make it a bit warmer. Leona and I weren't able to see the people speaking, but we could hear quite well most of the time. It was very special to be part of the crowd of Canadians who were honouring those who had fought for our country. After the ceremony, we looked at the wreaths that had been placed at the War Memorial and left our poppies on the Tomb of the Unknown Soldier.

Our next stop was Peterborough, Ontario. Ian was running in the Canadian College Athletic Association Cross-Country National Championships the next day. He was running for Team Ontario. Totally by coincidence, when I arrived at the event site, I parked my car next to his coach's car, which was very convenient. It was once again great to see students from all across the country. The weather was warmer than the day before. It was great day to be outdoors, to spend time with Ian, and to watch his race.

———

We didn't know it yet, but 2005 was our last Christmas together in Ontario. When we opened our gifts, Shadow kept us entertained. His antics brought back happy memories of our dear Syd. Shadow had missed Syd terribly initially but seemed to be more himself again. After Christmas, Leona went to a wedding shower for her friend Linda, who had moved to Calgary. After talking with Linda, Leona began to more seriously consider moving to Calgary. She thought there would be more job opportunities there, and she felt ready for a new beginning.

Ian, Leona, and I were once again invited to Dad and Mom's place for dinner on New Year's Day. We ate a bit late because Mom said she had forgotten to take meat out of the freezer. However, while Mom and I were doing dishes, I found thawed meat in two different places in her cupboards. I was very concerned and told my siblings about it. We were planning a family reunion in the summer as Dad and Mom would be celebrating their sixtieth anniversary in June. We prayed that Dad and Mom would still be able to live in their own apartment as their challenges in living on their own were increasing.

———

Soon, Leona decided that she would move to Calgary. Before her February departure, we visited Oma and celebrated Dad's eighty-fifth birthday. It was hard to see Leona go, but she deserved a new beginning. I also planned an April vacation to visit Leona and other family and friends in Alberta and British Columbia. It made saying goodbye easier.

That spring, I flew from London, Ontario, to Calgary, Alberta. I saw where Leona lived and noticed the afghan that Mom had crocheted for her on her bed, a reminder of her family that Leona saw every day. While Leona worked the next day, I took the CTrain (Calgary's rapid transit) downtown and did some exploring. I enjoyed the adventure of the day and didn't mind that I did it alone. At the end of the day, I met up with Leona, and we went back to her place together. She was enjoying the adventure of her new life.

The following day, my brother Len came from Rocky Mountain House so I could visit with him and his family for a few days. I hadn't spent one-on-one time with Len for many years, so our time together was very special. Seeing their acreage was like taking a deep breath. I was glad that Dad and Mom had been able to visit there the summer before.

After another short visit with Leona, I flew to Victoria, British Columbia, to visit Grace, who had been part of my Divorce Care group. She had very recently been diagnosed with lung cancer and appreciated the distraction of my visit as she showed me her favourite views. It was springtime in Victoria, with many blooming flowers and bushes and much beauty with the water and the mountains. One afternoon, I had coffee with my nephew Josh, who was a student at the University of Victoria.

From Victoria, I took the bus to Tsawwassen and left my luggage stored in the bus while I went on the ferry. It was a cool, windy, foggy day, but the natural rugged beauty of the shoreline was visible. It had been great to see the people I loved and cared about, but I enjoyed the time to be alone with my own thoughts, too.

I spent the next few days with my niece Marie, her husband, Matthew, and their wee son, Jacob, in their home in Surrey. My niece Jenn came to visit for a day as well. While on the mainland, we went to Fort Langley and Crescent Beach. British Columbia felt quite crowded, and I felt trapped between water and mountains. Those mountains seemed to be closing in on me. I remembered how I had also felt closed in when I went to the Rocky Mountains near Banff with Bob in 1980. I was glad I was going home to wider open spaces. It was exciting to think that I would have spring again once I returned to Ontario.

In March of 2004, more than two years before their sixtieth wedding anniversary, Mom had told me that the only gift she wanted was to have the whole family together. Matthew and Marie had already decided that they were bringing Jacob to Ontario. While I was in BC, I told Jenn and Josh that it would be special if they could be at the family reunion too. Our time together was a great opportunity to get to know Len's family better. The threads of their tapestries would one day mix through mine more regularly, once again a reminder that God knows the end from the beginning.

When I was back in Ontario and back to work, my parents' family doctor, Dr. Marcou, approached me. He had done memory tests on my parents, and he wanted me to go with them when they went for the results. Dr. Marcou was concerned that they might not remember what he told them. During that visit, Dad and Mom were told that they were both declining mentally, but they had strengths in different areas, and as long as there was no further decline in any area, they would be safe to remain living in their apartment. I'm not sure exactly how much my parents understood, but I know that they were pleased that nothing had to change.

Fortunately, Clarence, Mary, and I had already had end of life discussions with Dad and Mom, and they had signed forms for powers of attorney for personal care. It was good to know their wishes and for all of us to hear them speak the words. They had thought that a doctor would make the decision for them, but when they realized that they needed to make it themselves, they both chose a natural death, no resuscitation. Later that day, when Mom and I were travelling together in the car, she asked me if I was okay with their choice. I reassured her that of course it was okay if she wanted to go to heaven when given the opportunity.

———

Whew! Ian was finished his post-secondary education. Starting in September of 2000, first Ian and later Leona went away from home. My life felt busier during those years because of the driving I was doing on weekends when they came home. However, it was time well spent. I often had to work for part of the weekend, so I relished the time we spent talking in the car. The one-way drive alone was also often a blessing. When it was raining, it was extra cozy in the vehicle, a quiet time for worship and prayer. There were two worship CDs that I often played, and I sang along as I drove. When I prayed I sometimes used my prayer language when I didn't have the words to express my feelings.

There were many trips over the six years that Ian and Leona were away for school, first to the University of Waterloo and later to Humber College and Seneca College, both in Toronto. While Ian was in the co-op program there were also trips to his job placements. When I took him to Brampton, the Highway 401 was a sheet of ice for a long distance. All the cars were going very slowly, single file; any braking, and the car started skidding sideways. It took an hour to travel thirty-two kilometres. I was glad that Mary was with me. When I made trips for his Ottawa placement, I was rewarded with a chance to see the Christmas lights at the

Parliament Buildings. Beautifully done! I appreciate any opportunity to see Canada's great capital city!

I was pleased to attend Ian's graduation from Seneca College in June. It was the only post-secondary graduation ceremony either of my children attended. Ian had decided that he would move to Calgary as well and planned to share an apartment with Leona. He would wait until after we had the family reunion on the August long weekend. Together, Ian and I planned a yard sale to get rid of some extra furniture and other items I would no longer need once both Ian and Leona were no longer living at home. I decided to buy a car and let Ian take the van to Calgary with him. It would help with his move and also give him a vehicle.

June 14, 2006, was Dad and Mom's sixtieth anniversary. That morning, while drinking coffee on their patio, I mentioned to Dad that Ian and Leona had noticed how generous Grandpa was to Grandma. I asked Dad how he was able to give Mom everything she wanted. He answered, "She never asked me for anything I couldn't give her." It was teamwork at its finest and a great example of love and respect.

We had an open house on the anniversary day at Trillium Village where they lived. Dad had difficulty standing while receiving guests so sat on a barstool. I enjoyed seeing many friends and relatives and listening to all the memories that were shared. Dad and Mom had blessed many people by just being themselves. Mary and I had made up a few poster boards with various photographs. I wrote, "I'll always remember Dad and Mom looking at pictures on a display holding hands." Their love for each other truly blessed my life.

The open house was followed by preparation for the family reunion. There was much to do and many emotions to deal with. I had invited the eight members of Len's family to stay with us during the anniversary weekend. Ian was busy sorting through his belongings in preparation for his move. He stored his things in the workshop downstairs, as we needed his bedroom for guests. Besides my busy time at home, I sometimes had busy shifts at work. On one of those busy days I wrote, "43C humidex. I got stomach cramps just walking home from work; taking Imovane and Xanax to help with sleep; and I feel like I'm missing the whole summer. It's been so busy getting ready for various things."

Ready or not, events were unfolding for our August long weekend family reunion and anniversary celebration. Leona flew in from Calgary on Thursday evening. On Friday morning, a day before the first anniversary of Syd's death, Ian, Leona, and I spread Syd's ashes. We drove to the edge of town where Ian and Leona had taken the leash off of Syd if they went running with him. It was where he had been allowed to run free. Syd was free from pain forever and was now living on in our memories. It was good to spend time together as we remembered Syd.

Friday afternoon, Len's family settled into our home. It was my youngest niece's eleventh birthday, and her sisters wanted to give Kristin a special birthday supper. I supplied bowls and dishes, and they bought the food. Dad and Mom joined us that evening as well. It was a great way for my parents to spend more time with their "far-away" family. We set tables up in the backyard and had a picnic. That night, there were eleven people sleeping in my house.

Dad and Mom's anniversary gift was a family project, put together by Mary, Jeri, and me. We made a calendar to help them remember family birthdays and anniversaries. Making a calendar like this has become much simpler over the years, but back then, we either didn't know how or didn't care. We spent a day in Hamilton cutting paper, pasting on stickers, scanning pictures, and putting it all together. We had a theme for each month, an individual picture of each person for their birthday month, and a wedding picture of each couple on their anniversary month. We had a lot of fun that day, and Dad and Mom were thrilled with their gift when they received it.

Dad and Mom's family had grown to thirty-two people, and they all came to the reunion. Several activities were planned for people to interact and have fun together. Dad and Mom seemed a bit overwhelmed by all the activity but enjoyed themselves immensely. At our barbeque on Saturday, they sat on the edge of the crowd beaming as they watched all their children, grandchildren, and great-grandchildren interacting with each other.

On Sunday morning, many of us went to the church with Dad and Mom. Later we had a picnic in a local park where the children enjoyed playing on the playground equipment and the adults had another opportunity to mingle and spend just a bit more time with family they might not see in a long time. After the picnic, it was time for people to catch flights or to start the drive home. It had been a great time and was over much too soon. All the thought and preparation had been more than worth it!

Ian, Leona, and I returned home after the family picnic to pack the van for Ian's departure to Calgary the next day. He planned to camp as he crossed the country, so we had to be sure he could get at the things he needed for that. It was a busy afternoon and evening. I'm sure Ian was glad to sleep in his own bed again for his last evening at home. Leona's return flight to Calgary was at seven the next morning. At 5 a.m., Leona and I headed to the airport in my car, and Ian left for Calgary in the van that was now his.

Goodbyes were hard for me that morning. I didn't feel like they were running away from me. I knew it was good that they were taking the opportunity to move forward with their lives. Leona was returning to her job. Ian was starting on a new adventure and would meet up with Leona in a few days. It was hard not to think of myself. My losses had come in half-year increments. First Syd had died, then Leona moved to Calgary, and now Ian was leaving too. Life was a big mystery sometimes, and that could be stressful, but there was the reassurance that God was in control!

My trip back from the airport was made a bit easier because I knew that my nephew Ryan planned to visit that afternoon. Later, Tim, his brother, joined us. It was great spending time with them and a great distraction from the huge difference in the house after the busyness of the previous few weeks. The next day I washed sheets and hung them out to dry and called Ian's aunt in Saskatchewan to let her know that he was travelling across the country and hoped to visit them. I no longer needed the sports channels for Ian and Leona, so I changed the TV plan to basic. I wanted to be able to talk for longer periods on the phone, so I got a North America phone plan. The cost was about the same. Shadow the cat and I were ready for the next phase of our lives.

———

Mary and I decided we deserved another road trip after the busyness associated with the reunion. This time we circled Lake Erie. There were more industries and inhabited places than there had been around Lake Superior. As we travelled along and saw more and more towns, we thought that certainly we should be able to find a Dairy Queen. It became the quest on our journey. Finally we found one when we were almost back home. After the busyness at the beginning of the summer, it was good to enjoy these relaxing summer days close to the water.

A few weeks later, Dad's sister and her husband came to visit, still in celebration of Dad and Mom's sixtieth anniversary. Dad, Mom, Mary, and I took them to Niagara Falls. We took advantage of Dad's handicapped status and parked quite close to the falls. We also visited an aunt who lived in the Shalom Gardens apartments (assisted living), connected to Shalom Manor. Mary and I hoped that by seeing the assisted living apartments, Dad and Mom might realize that it would be a good time for them to make a change in their living arrangements, but they didn't seem to be looking for a change.

———

The Royal Doulton Petite Figure of the Year in 2006 was named "Mary." I thought of a meaningful way to give "Mary" to Mary, so I called my niece. On my sister's birthday, her mother, her sister, her daughter, and her two granddaughters gave her a "Petite Mary" figurine. It had been a bit of a challenge for Mom to understand the significance of the people involved with Mary's gift, but she gladly gave me some money. The next day, I walked over to visit with Dad and Mom. I wrote, "They were walking outside—what an old couple. Dad with his walker—Mom looking vaguely about. I wonder how much longer they will be able to live in their apartment."

———

It was time to consider some repairs that needed to be done to the house and outside. I had some very basic skills, and Ian had helped me replace some light fixtures, but it was difficult for me to maintain a house on my own. With the help of professionals and others, I already had the furnace replaced and added air conditioning, replaced the toilets and sinks in both bathrooms, had the shingles on the roof replaced, and had various areas painted.

I had managed to make one change that tested the limits of my abilities. There was carpeting on a wall in our lower level family room, probably for soundproofing. I took the carpet off and replaced it with panelling. I did all the measuring, cut the holes in the right places for the electrical outlets, nailed the panelling in place, and replaced the trim. The fun part of the project was when I bought the panelling. I had measured the length the panels needed to be and asked the men at the lumberyard to cut off the bottom piece so there would be one less step for me. When the panels were placed in the back of my van, they fit perfectly. One of the men got a strange look on his face and asked, "You didn't ask us to cut these panels just so they would fit in your van, did you?" I emphatically said, "No," and I smiled my sweetest smile.

Now, in the fall of 2006, nothing needed to be done urgently, but I couldn't ignore needed repairs indefinitely. It seemed like a lot to do for "just me." With Ian and Leona so far away, there wouldn't be weekend visits, and perhaps not extended visits either. I briefly considered the possibility of sharing my home with someone, but I decided the house wasn't suitable for sharing, especially as I was a shift worker. Was it time for a change in where I lived?

One Sunday I began speaking my prayer language during one of the songs; it just came up and out. In that moment, God reminded me that He knew the words of my heart even when I didn't. Within a week, I took the first step forward in finding a "start over" place. After discussing the idea with my family, I put my house up for sale, and I prayed that some worthy family would buy it. "God doesn't leave us with a giant goal or a great plan. He provides direction for all of the small steps that are necessary for getting to the big goal."[5]

——————

Very shortly after I put the house up for sale, on October 6, 2006, Dad had a stroke and was taken to a hospital in London by ambulance. Mom and I followed in my car. I had to make the decision about whether Dad would receive a clot-busting drug or not, as Mom was too frazzled to decide, and there was no time to contact my siblings. The drug could either kill Dad or, hopefully, make him better. A doctor helped me make the decision when he heard that Dad did not wish to have his life prolonged by artificial means. He said, "He wouldn't want to be left this way." I had to agree. Dad was looking, but not seeing us, not responding in any way. Was he in there? I gave permission for Dad to receive the drug. I was very relieved when Clarence arrived to be with Mom and me.

The stroke was the change Dr. Marcou had talked about. Dad and Mom could no longer live independently. Those were difficult weeks. Mom was not coping well. Stress and anxiety were making her more confused. It wasn't possible to talk with her about plans for the future. She wanted them both to stay in their apartment, but that wasn't going to be possible anymore.

One evening when I visited Dad, he was sitting on his hospital bed looking very sad. When I asked him what was wrong, he said, "Now I can't give her what she wants anymore." Dad's faith and trust in God were strong, and he trusted that, in time, Mom would adapt to the changes that

---

5 Charles Stanley, *The Source of My Strength* [Nashville, Tennessee: Thomas Nelson, 1994], 155

were needed. He had seen my mother's strength through the loss of her first child, immigration to Canada, and a few previous moves.

During his time in the hospital, Dad recovered most of his abilities. He was left with some swallowing problems, which required special food preparation. On a one-day pass from the hospital, Dad went with me to the vehicle registration office, and the ownership of their car was transferred to me. In mid-November, after *many* anxious moments and frustrating events, my siblings and I, working together, were able to move Dad and Mom into assisted living at the Shalom Gardens apartments. They would now live a two-hour drive away from me instead of a short walk away.

I was sick and exhausted with all the changes and busyness and had missed some shifts at work; too much was happening too quickly. The sale of the house had been put on hold, but those changes would still be coming. Most of what happened was beyond my control, so I could only try to absorb and react properly to as many of the events as I could. None of this was hidden from God. I had to remember that God is God and He loves me more than I will ever be able to understand. But—wow!

———

During that time, there was one very enjoyable distraction, a reminder that God was weaving my tapestry and had wonderful surprises in store for me. A few years earlier, I had joined Meet Christians (MC), an online community with active forums. During quiet times at home I enjoyed connecting with people from North America, Australia, and Europe. Now two of my MC friends were coming from Virginia to take a friend from Australia to see Niagara Falls. They wondered if they could meet a few "Ontario girls" in Burlington, Ontario, for dinner. It was a great opportunity for a new adventure in friendship. Kim and Sharyn lived in Virginia, but Sharyn was an Aussie. In the end, the other two "Ontario girls" weren't able to come. I not only met Kim and Sharyn for dinner but also went to see Niagara Falls at night with them and their guest. Great new friendships were formed. My evening had been an awesome haven in the midst of the challenges my siblings and I faced after Dad's stroke.

The second weekend in December, I flew to Calgary to spend four days with Ian and Leona. They had been sharing a two-bedroom apartment since very shortly after Ian's arrival in Alberta. I would have an early Christmas celebration in Calgary and be back in Ontario for Christmas with my family there. It was great to see Ian and Leona and their "new world" for a few days. It was also an adjustment, as I was now a visitor in their home. They were doing a fine job of caring for themselves and their apartment, and they didn't need interference from me. We had a Christmas dinner with all the trimmings and exchanged our gifts. We also drove to Rocky Mountain House to visit with Len and his family. It was good to know that some family members were that close if Ian and Leona needed them.

Life was still busy during the remaining days of December. I continued to have house showings and looked for a townhouse or condo to buy, and Mary and I spent time sorting through Dad's and Mom's things that were still in their Strathroy apartment. Initially one or both of us made the two-hour drive to Grimsby quite regularly. I was disappointed to discover that I seldom felt like I had the energy to make the drive alone. I had driven Ian and Leona to and from school many times over the years, but somehow this trip was different. Perhaps it was because I was driving both ways alone and going to and from an empty house. Perhaps I was still affected by all the challenges and changes of the previous months.

Christmas Day 2006 started at Ed and Mary's home. I had been invited for an overnight visit so I wouldn't be alone on Christmas morning. It was a great idea! Later, we had "Batterink Christmas" in Hamilton at Clarence's home. Dad and Mom were able to join us. Dad was not impressed when we cut his turkey into tiny pieces. He had thought he'd be able to eat "normal" food for the day. It had been a good decision to be in Calgary earlier in the month and now spend time with my parents and other family.

During these years of "becoming me," God gave me several adventures. Meeting Jurgen had given me a little push into my future as that experience helped me to stop looking back. I travelled on my own and did road trips with Mary and Leona, and I was much more involved in family events. My nursing colleagues said I was having too much fun!

There had also been stressful times. Ian, Leona, and I had conversations that were tough but necessary and beneficial. I experienced the loss of our beloved Syd; Leona and Ian moved to Calgary; and my parents' role in my life changed dramatically. These events were not of my choosing, but they helped me to be able to focus on myself in a positive way. I began to see myself apart from my roles as a mother and a daughter. I enjoyed more of the present and started looking towards a different future. I remembered how I had been blessed many times by being aware of the joy of the Lord in my life. I looked forward to 2007 with hope.

chapter thirteen

ON MY OWN AGAIN—
GETTING COMFORTABLE

*Being confident of this, that he who began a good work in you will carry
it on to completion until the day of Christ Jesus.*

—Philippians 1:6

EARLY IN THE NEW YEAR, A WORTHY FAMILY BOUGHT MY HOUSE. THIS WAS AN
answer to the prayer I had prayed when I put it up for sale. I decided to
rent an apartment rather than buy something. It was a busy and challenging time, sorting through all the things and furniture I had and deciding
what to do with everything. Once my decisions were made, it was a challenge to make sure everything ended up where I wanted it to be.

First, I selected what I wanted to keep. Next, I asked the new
owners if they would like to have any of the furniture, and those pieces
stayed in the house. Then I decided which things would be appropriate
for the girls group at church to sell at their yard sale. Lastly, anything
that was left was taken by the movers to a local reservation, to be distrib-
uted among people there. In the months ahead, I would marvel that I
didn't seem to be missing anything I needed.

The day after the house sold, I was told about an apartment that
would be perfect for me. It was the lower level of a quadruplex. It was
bright and airy with two bedrooms, spacious enough for my piano and
small freezer, and in a good neighbourhood. The living space was a
large square that was great for entertaining. There was enough space for
me to have my large table with all its extensions in it. I had an outdoor
patio area and a clothesline that I could use, even though I had a washer
and dryer.

Ed and Jeri helped Shadow and me to get settled into our new home one February day. I don't think Shadow ever liked that apartment too much. He would sometimes disappear for a few days at a time. His life had changed a lot in the previous two years too. First, he experienced the death of his great friend Syd and then the disappearance of Ian and Leona. Shadow and I lived well alongside of each other, but we were never buddies.

I settled into my new place quite easily. Thick frost, snow, and freezing rain initiated my first days of driving to work. It had been great to be able to walk to work for seven years, and I had wondered how much I would stress out about the weather now that I had to drive. It was good to discover so soon that it wasn't an issue at all. House and yard maintenance were no longer issues either. When I had a problem at the apartment, I just needed to call Mike, the maintenance man. I knew Mike well because he had been on Team Honduras with me. It was a great "start over" place. God's provision was beyond my expectations.

———

As I settled into my less stressful lifestyle, I began to take better care of myself physically. Leona had given me a strength-training program before she moved to Calgary, and I did the exercises more often. I walked regularly, and I did a lot of research into how to eat better to control my weight. I lost weight and felt better about myself than I had in a long time. I was starting to find "me" in a whole new way, and it was good.

My new place was great for entertaining. I sometimes had the UFO ladies or my YaYa friends at my apartment for supper or for an evening of fellowship. This was awesome for me to experience. During my marriage, Bob had told me that I wasn't able to be a good hostess. I had tried inviting people over but soon limited our visitors to family and close friends. Now when I was the hostess, people were having fun times filled with lots of sharing and laughter.

Another team was planning to go to Honduras, and initially I planned to go too. With difficulty and some negative feelings that I had to work through, I decided not to go. I went with my gut even though I didn't fully understand my decision. In hindsight, I realize that going to Honduras wasn't in God's plan for me. The plans for my life changed drastically over the next months. God knew the end from the beginning.

That summer, Len's daughter, Jenn, was getting married in Rocky Mountain House, Alberta. Ed and Mary invited me to travel to Calgary with them in their Roadtrek. We travelled through the United States, stopping to see their son Ryan and his family in Iowa, the Corn Palace in Mitchell, South Dakota, Mount Rushmore, the Chief Sitting Bull Monument, and the Badlands, also in South Dakota, and Glacier National Park in Montana. God's touch in nature and in the creative gifts given to so many was awesome to see. There was beauty everywhere: across the flat land, as we approached mountains, in the interesting layers of rock in the Badlands, and even in the wide open sky above.

As we drove across South Dakota, Mary, Ed, and I saw one sign after another for Wall Drugs in Wall, South Dakota. Mary and I decided we had seen enough signs and didn't need to or want to go to Wall Drugs. However, when we saw a sign that advertised homemade ice cream, Ed's one vote was more powerful than our two votes, and we had to stop there. On the Wall Drugs website, it's advertised as being a 76,000 square foot wonderland of free attractions. It actually was a very interesting stop, and the ice cream was delicious. It was the perfect day for ice cream as well, as the temperature was 102°F or almost 39°C.

Leona worked at Kilkenny's, an Irish pub, and was excited that she had saved enough vouchers to take all of her family out for supper after our arrival in Calgary. Clarence and Jeri had arrived in Alberta for the wedding as well. There were seven of us in a private room sharing Leona's treat. Her gift to us was appreciated. I visited with Ian and Leona for a few days, attended the wedding with them, and then flew back to Ontario. It had been good to see so many family members again. This was the first family wedding my parents were unable to attend, and we missed them. In September, when Clarence's daughter got married in Ontario, Dad and Mom enjoyed the festivities. It was hard to watch their slow mental and physical decline.

In October of 2006, I had talked to Pastor Fred about starting a grief support group at our church, and in the spring I had met with Lydia, who was interested in helping set up a group. In late summer of 2007, we found out that a local church had the Grief Share videos, and we would be able to use those. Lydia and I acted as co-leaders. I would miss some sessions because of work. We met once a week between September 24 and December 5. I was able to share how I had been able to find hope and joy after loss too. My personal experience had been loss through divorce, but I also had insights gained through my nursing career. We ended our sessions with a Christmas dinner at my place. It was good to have everyone around my table that evening and to know that everyone had benefited from being part of the group.

I had missed a Grief Share session in the fall when I took a few days to drive south to visit my "Meet Christian" friends Kim and Sharyn in Virginia. On this trip, too, there was much beautiful nature to see. The leaves were changing to their fall colours, which added to the magnificence. I enjoyed staying with Kim and meeting her family. Kim, Sharyn, and I also did some sightseeing. The Blue Ridge Parkway was especially lovely. The mountains there were very different from the Rockies near Calgary. It was another example of the variety that God creates in all things. I took a different route home and stopped to see Dad and Mom.

Life was changing positively in many ways, but I was still feeling restless. It was a lonely feeling being the only family member in town when Ed and Mary were gone to visit their children. At one time I had thought of buying a house in a university town that I could share with students, but that scenario made no sense to me now. Also, even ten years after the end of my marriage, people still asked me how Bob was doing. Our lives were very separate by this point, and saying "I don't know" sounded too much like "I don't care," so I never knew what to say.

When I considered moving to Calgary, it felt like a great idea. Not only would I be nearer to Ian and Leona, I would also have a fresh start. I was glad when Ian and Leona liked the idea. We had the understanding that they would be free to move away from Calgary any time one or both of them wanted to. This was more than an adventure; it would start a different section of my tapestry.

———

Even though I didn't intend to move until the spring, I started the job search process that fall. Once again I went to Calgary in early December to celebrate Christmas. While I was there, I got an email from a job recruiter. When she realized that I was actually in Calgary at the time, she set me up for an interview the next day. The manager and assistant manager I met were very friendly and easy to talk to. I liked that a lot. I was surprised that they were willing to hire me in December even though I didn't want to start working until mid-May. It was great to return home with a sound job offer, which was very soon confirmed. I would be working on a respiratory medicine–thoracic surgery unit at Foothills Hospital. Respiratory medicine was familiar territory for me. Thoracic surgery would be an exciting challenge, I thought.

———

I knew I would no longer be an active part of Dad's and Mom's lives when I lived in Alberta. There might not be many more birthdays and anniversaries to celebrate, but I might miss the ones that still happened. It was hard to focus on myself, but I felt a need to move forward with my life. Dad and Mom had been younger when they had made their decision to move away from their parents. When I told them about my decision to move, Dad said, "You can't transplant an old tree, but I don't think you're too old to be transplanted." Mom said, "I thought you should go. Your kids are there." It was good to have their approval.

I knew there would also be many other changes for me. I would miss other family events that happened in Ontario: weddings, birthdays, and funerals. I would be leaving my friends, my church family, and my job. I had lived in the same community and worked at the same hospital for more than twenty years. Many of the nurses I had started working with in 1986 were still there. It was easy to say that I was only a plane flight away, but the reality was that there would be a great disconnect between my past and my future.

Living and working in a small community were interesting, and I would miss seeing familiar faces so regularly. When I went to the store to pick up a few things, it sometimes took me a long time to return home. I told Ian and Leona that it didn't matter how many things I had to pick up; it depended on who I met when I was out. One time a former patient was behind me in line at the grocery store. When he recognized me, he said, "Oh, it's you! I didn't recognize you with clothes on." Yikes! That took a bit of explaining to all the other customers within hearing distance.

While working at the hospital, I often looked after people who were from my church. One of the nurses asked me if I was related to everyone in Strathroy. I answered that there were lots of people in my church family. Through the years, I was able to support many families when their loved ones died. It was always a humbling experience when I was allowed to share this intimate family time. Sometimes I was able to help family members understand the different ways of grieving as they struggled to understand someone else's behaviour. Would I ever have an opportunity for those close relationships with patients and families again?

In February, before I left Ontario, Ian came for a visit. He wanted to visit Bob and my parents and see my apartment. Soon after, Shadow and I had a quick trip to Calgary on a very cheap flight. Leona had found an apartment where she could have a pet and was very glad to have her cat back with her. While I was there, with Ian's help I was able to find a two-bedroom apartment in a small building in a great location in northwest Calgary. In May I could start my new job and move into my new place. It was a blessing to have these details finalized.

I got a $5,000 relocation bonus from Alberta, so most of my moving expenses were paid for. There was still much sorting and packing to do. I had furniture, books, and other items that weren't worth taking across the country, so I had to distribute those things somewhere. There were decisions Ian and Leona had to make, too. Most of their boxed items had gone to Calgary when Mary's son Jon moved there. Now they had to decide if they still wanted some items of furniture that I had stored for them.

There were many goodbyes. I had several gatherings with family and friends before I left. I still treasure my gifts and the comments from the nurses I worked with for many years. I wrote, "I've worked my last shift at SMGH. There will be a lifetime of memories—but no regrets about leaving the job. There are people I will miss—some I know I may never see again. It is good to have the certainty that I am doing the right thing." I knew my Divorce Care friends and YaYa friends would be irreplaceable. I didn't want to repeat the journey I had gone through with them, but I had been blessed to have them in my life to share that time with.

When it was time to leave Ontario, it was especially hard to say goodbye to Dad and Mom. I'm not sure Mom fully comprehended what was happening even though she had told me that I belonged where Ian and Leona were. I was sad when Dad said to me, "Maybe I will never see you again." After immigrating to Canada, Dad and Mom had never seen Mom's parents or Dad's mother again. I certainly was planning to fly back for visits, but I was leaving elderly parents, and anything could happen. I knew from my years of nursing that life changes can come suddenly, and I had prepared myself for that.

On April 25, the moving van arrived. It was a busy day. I liked seeing how carefully my possessions were handled. The driver of the van would unload in Calgary, so I would see him again. It was good to know that I would see a familiar face in a new place. Soon I was sitting on the floor of an empty apartment. I was tired. I was also excited. This was the end of a chapter of my life, and I was looking forward to new beginnings. I picked up my purse, locked the door for the last time, and dropped off the keys on the way to Mary's house.

As I got more comfortable with "me," I began making choices that allowed big changes to happen. First, I rented an apartment instead of buying a place to live. Second, I dared to plan a new start elsewhere. It was the beginning of new life in me. My move was about God's plan for me, not God's plan for Ian, Leona, and me together. I was looking forward to a new and different relationship with my adult children. I was confident that God was with me and I was not stepping into the great unknown alone.

chapter fourteen
CALGARY

May the God of hope fill you with all joy and peace as you trust in him,
so that you may overflow with hope by the power of the Holy Spirit.
—Romans 15:13

MARY OFFERED TO HELP ME WITH THE DRIVE WEST. IT WOULD BE OUR "SISTERS'
outing" for that year. I spent my last weekend in Strathroy, at Mary's home.
We left on the morning of April 28. We had a deadline to meet. I had an
appointment to have phone, cable, and Internet installed at my Calgary
apartment on the afternoon of May 1. My belongings would arrive sometime between May 2 and May 9. I had specifically chosen to move this late
in the spring because I didn't want to have any problems with snow.

In northern Ontario, we were surprised that the traffic was very
sparse for a while. When we stopped to eat, we were told that the highway had just been opened again. It had been closed because of a snowstorm. We were fortunate not to have been delayed. We had little time for
extended stops but took our friend Margo out for lunch when we went
through Thunder Bay. Unfortunately, when we got to Calgary the afternoon of May 1, we found out that the phone, cable, and Internet installer
had been there in the morning. I had to wait a full week to get service.
Thankfully I had my cellphone so could still connect with Ian and Leona.
However, I still had an Ontario phone number, so we didn't talk often.

On arrival day, Mary went to visit her son Jon and his wife, who
also lived in Calgary. Ian, Leona, and I celebrated my arrival by going to
Denny's for supper. It was the first of several suppers there. Ian worked
nights, and he enjoyed going to a place that served all-day breakfast. My
second day in Calgary was another celebration. It was Len's birthday. Ed,

who had flown in from Ontario, Mary, and I drove to Rocky Mountain House to take Len out for lunch.

We went to The Crossing in Banff National Park. Len had taken Dad and Mom there for lunch on their last trip west in 2005, so there was a bit of sentiment attached to our destination. It was a glorious sunny day, and the mountain scenery was amazing! It was interesting to feel insignificant because of the grandeur of the mountains yet so significant because the God who created and formed it all loves me! It was a great twenty-four hours of blending family and nature, the two blessings that were mine during my time in Alberta.

My first day of work was scheduled for May 12, so I hoped to be well settled into my apartment by then. I had packed lawn chairs, a cot, and various household items in the car so I could survive in my apartment until the moving van arrived. However, my things didn't arrive until May 9. With few personal items and no Internet or phone, it was a tough start. Soon I was adjusting to my new job while trying to make my new apartment feel like home. I went to each orientation shift more tired than the shift before, and I was more overwhelmed than I had imagined I could be.

A new province meant new licence plates, a new health card, a new driver's licence, and new insurance for home and car. A new city meant a new bank location, a new grocery store, a new route to work, and looking for a new church. I have a terrible sense of direction, so I got lost so many times that I felt like crying. It was good when Leona was my passenger as she knew her way around the city quite well. I often remembered that Dad had said he didn't think I was too old to be transplanted and that Mom thought I should be nearer to Ian and Leona. It was tough but worthwhile, as I was looking for a "new Annette" too.

In the first few months I visited various churches of a few different denominations, and then I decided to join Maranatha Christian Reformed Church in northwest Calgary. The deciding factor for me was when an older woman sitting in front of me found the Scripture passage the pastor was going to read and handed that Bible back to me. I soon found out that there were many other ways the members of Maranatha worked to be "God's ambassadors." I enjoyed being part of their church family, and I was surprised that it was a great place to play Dutch Bingo.

There were several connections to Strathroy and one to Hamilton. These threads, connecting my past to my present, added colourful designs to my tapestry. They made the unfamiliar feel much more familiar.

———•———

I had a phone conversation with Bob shortly after I arrived in Calgary. I don't remember why we spoke, but it wasn't a good conversation. Bob once again blamed my parents for our divorce, and I hung up on him. After that, Ian asked me not to speak with Bob any more, as it only made the situation more difficult for him. It was a request that I honoured. In later times, if Bob called Ian on his cellphone when I was present, Ian never mentioned that he was with me. It made me sad that Bob and I couldn't even communicate as parents, but it was best for me to accept the way things were.

———•———

Shortly after I arrived in Calgary, Ian moved into a one-bedroom apartment as Leona was no longer living with him. At my apartment, I missed having an outdoor space. Ian liked my place very much as there were several paths nearby for walking and running. I suggested that he take over my apartment, and I would find another place. It was a win-win situation that my landlord approved of. So, eight months after arriving in Calgary, I moved into a totally renovated two-bedroom basement apartment. Only one person lived upstairs, and I had the patio and a storage area in the backyard for my use.

One challenge was that the new apartment was smaller. When Bob and I had built our house, I had done a lot of measuring of walls and furniture so we would be able to place our furniture where we wanted to. Now I carefully measured furniture and walls and had a very organized plan. However, on moving day, I discovered that I hadn't figured out ceiling height or angles in the hallway. After a few anxious moments I realized that the necessary plan was better than "my" plan. It was all good! Later, I even found room for the electronic piano I bought.

Northwest Calgary is in the foothills, so walking is great exercise, as the terrain is quite hilly. From where I lived, I could walk to see views of downtown Calgary and the Rocky Mountains and to an outdoor skating rink in winter. Calgary is the sunniest city in Canada, and I thoroughly enjoyed all that sunshine! In the winter, when nights were cold and days were sunny, the sidewalks often got very slippery. However, the official walking paths were kept clear. Winter weather could be very cold or quite mild when the chinooks brought warm winds.

———

I worked with care aides for the first time in my career at Foothills Hospital. Initially, I had problems figuring out our roles. Was I expecting too much of them? Was I doing too much patient care myself and missing other things I was expected to do? When I didn't do the care, I missed the opportunity to assess my patients, not only their physical health but their emotional health too. As I adjusted to routines, I found more time to do care myself, asking for help with the tasks I couldn't do alone. I discovered that co-operation and communication are needed no matter which model of nursing care is used.

Sadly, this job wasn't working out well for me. I was working eight-hour shifts again, but only day and night shifts. When I accepted that schedule, I thought it would be great to have my evenings off all the time. But I didn't sleep well when I worked nights, and all my time was consumed with working or recovering from work. Also, it was challenging being an experienced nurse in a new position. There were many new policies and procedures to learn. The other experienced nurses had high expectations, and there were many new staff nurses on the unit who expected me to be able to answer their questions. I often didn't know where to go to get *my* questions answered. I was stressed and tired.

I remembered a conversation I had with Dad when I was still in my first nursing job. One morning as I was leaving for work, Dad said, "Have fun!" When I replied that I was on my way to work, he said, "If you're not going to have fun, you should find something else to do." For a long time I hadn't had the freedom or option to make a choice. Now I was thinking about an exit plan. When I told my manager I was leaving because I wasn't having fun, he kindly said, "You have to remember you aren't sixteen anymore, Dorothy." I decided that I would quit my job before my fifty-fifth birthday in February and then take a month off to travel to Virginia and Ontario.

———

Early in 2009, I got a phone call that Dad's health was failing rapidly. I made the decision not to go to Ontario right away, even though I knew that I might not see Dad alive again. I had been in Ontario for Mom's birthday at the end of October, and it had been good to spend time with Dad and Mom then. On the final evening of that visit, one of my siblings took a photo of me with my parents. It was the last picture of the three of us together.

On January 16, I received the news that the family had been called to the nursing home as Dad's condition had deteriorated further. Len and I met at the Calgary airport and sat next to each other on the next flight to Hamilton. During our flight almost everyone was talking and reading about a plane with 155 people on board that had ditched into a chilly Hudson River the day before. The news didn't bother us. We were thinking about Dad and our family in Ontario. When we arrived at midnight, Clarence met us at the airport and told us that Dad had died two hours earlier.

Dear Dad—February 3, 1921–January 16, 2009

Dad's body was still in his own bed when we got to the nursing home. He had a very peaceful look on his face with his mouth slightly open. It was like his spirit had gone from here to heaven with his last breath! I felt blessed that I got to see him before his body was moved. While I still worked in Ontario I had worried that Dad might die sometime when I was working nights. The hospital would surely move Dad's body to the morgue before I had a chance to arrive. Now, I lived in Calgary and had to fly to Ontario, and God had worked it all out—a brilliant thread in my tapestry!

At the nursing home, Dad and Mom each had a bed in sections of a shared room. Mom was experiencing some symptoms of dementia. She was asleep the evening that Dad died, so the decision was made to tell her about Dad's death after she woke up. I was given a mattress on the floor next to Dad's bed so I would be there if Mom woke up during the night. Early in the morning, after I told her that Dad had died, she asked me to crawl into her nursing home bed with her. She would talk a little, pat my cheek and tell me how wonderful her children were, and then repeat the same actions. After a while she told me I'd better leave and get some more sleep. I could soon hear her gentle snores.

At Dad's funeral, my niece Heather read the memories of the twelve grandchildren. Ian's memory: "My best memories of Grandpa are of the times I stopped by when they lived at Trillium Village. It was the quiet time shared looking out the window, talking about the world as it went by. He was very observant and noticed many interesting things." Leona's memory: "I remember one Sunday at church we had a sending off for all the students heading out to college and university. All the students were invited to the front, and then a parent was asked to come to the front to bless the students. Since I didn't have a parent there that day, both Uncle Ed and Grandpa stood up. Grandpa was insistent that he come to the front. He struggled to the front of the church, walking with his cane, and stood while the blessing for the students was read. We walked back to the pew together."

I loved hearing about the many ways in which Dad had touched the lives of many other people, just by being himself. My memories weren't spoken aloud, but I remembered when Dad prayed for me on my birthday. I remembered when one of Dad's friends who was a patient asked me if I knew how proud Dad was of me. I remembered Dad's unique hugs; he would enfold me with his right arm and, because of his fused left wrist, would just press his left arm into my back. My children and I had felt Dad's love and care for us. I was blessed to be the daughter of a great earthly father, a man who lived his faith and who showed by example that he trusted his Father God. I will love you forever, Dad!

Later, when I was leaving Ontario for Alberta, it was good to know that I already had plans to be in Ontario in early March. I would see Mom again then. Back in Alberta, I handed in my official resignation at my job and started a search for something that would suit me better. Soon, Mary and Ed were in Calgary for the birth of Jon's son. They extended their stay to take Ian, Leona, and I out for breakfast on the morning of my fifty-fifth birthday. When I left for my vacation a few days later, I didn't have another job. I would continue my search after I returned.

I flew to Roanoke, Virginia, with a stopover at the busy O'Hare airport in Chicago. After I visited with Kim's family for a few days, Kim, Sharyn, and I took a road trip. In West Virginia, I enjoyed meeting Kim's parents and seeing where she used to live. In Pennsylvania, we visited Amish towns in Lancaster County. It was great to spend time with my American and Aussie sisters again.

After another stopover in O'Hare, I flew to Toronto for the Ontario part of my trip. I spent a few days with my niece Heather and her family, with Clarence and Jeri, and with Ed and Mary. During this longer visit I visited some friends, went to the Grand Theatre with Mary, and went to the sugar bush for pancakes and maple syrup. It was a bit ironic that I had to visit Ontario from Calgary before having a sugar bush outing. I had great visits with Mom during that time. She even asked me about their car, which was now my car. I wrote, "The last day was awesome. She hardly repeated herself, she remembered things she hadn't remembered in a long time, and she had more energy."

This good visit with Mom reminded me of Opa, my paternal grandfather. He had visited from the Netherlands for three months in 1960 and for a shorter time when I was fifteen years old. He was not a very happy man and didn't seem too interested in having a relationship with his Canadian grandchildren. Later, when I was twenty-three years old, visiting in the Netherlands, and Opa had some dementia, he and I had a great visit. I could speak some Dutch at the time, and he had stories to tell about his last visit to Canada. He remembered how much I liked to curl up with a book. As a young adult, I was able to feel affection towards him, and I was glad that I hadn't given up on having a relationship with the only grandparent I ever met.

———•———

When I arrived back in Calgary, there was a message on my answering machine, inviting me to set up an interview at Bow-Crest, a long-term care facility. I soon started another job, working on a seventy-seven bed dementia unit. As I was adjusting to my new job, I was also having a challenge adjusting to being at home alone after being with people for four weeks. I started looking at profiles at the Christian Café.

Two days later, I found "Good Guy" (Max) from Surrey BC to connect with. Our first emails were about our thoughts on "Be still and know that I am God" from Psalm 46, and we continued on from there. I enjoyed our ongoing conversation.

At work, it took a while for me to learn the names and faces of all the residents who were not able to identify themselves. This was especially important when giving out medications. Soon I knew their names and their personalities and how to best approach each person. I worked all afternoon shifts, 3 p.m. to 11 p.m., so I was there at suppertime and when the residents got settled for bed. There were almost a dozen care aides and only two professional staff (RN/LPN) on the unit on evenings, so my role was also supervisory. The shifts I worked were chaotic at times but challenging, rewarding, and fun too.

———•———

My mother was right; I belonged closer to my children. In Calgary, we became a family of three in a different, better way. We were all focusing on moving forward with our lives, creating a new normal for ourselves. We had our own jobs and our own routines, so we didn't have too many opportunities to be a threesome, but it was good when we did. To celebrate Mother's Day one year, we made six lasagnas. We spent time mixing and chopping, talking and laughing. We ate supper together and divided the remaining lasagnas among us.

I had my first experience of hiking a mountain trail the day Ian, Leona, and I went to Johnston Canyon and Castle Mountain, both in Banff National Park. I found out that climbing up Castle Mountain was the easy part. Coming down, my knees got very sore. I could hardly get back to the car. I probably looked like a wimp, but each step was a gutsy move as it hurt so much. The pain was all worth it though because the views from "way up there" had been great. And it wasn't my last mountain hike.

Ian, Leona, and I took the C-train when we went to the rodeo at the Calgary Stampede, "The Greatest Outdoor Show on Earth." The rodeo is one of the largest and the most famous event of its kind in the world. Like most people in the crowd, we wore our cowboy hats. The agricultural exhibitions on the stampede grounds were very interesting for this former farm girl. During Stampede Week, I had fun dressing in western clothing for shopping, work, and church.

I had outings with Ian and Leona individually as well. For Leona and me, it was mainly shopping and going out for supper. Ian and I visited Bob's sister in Moose Jaw, and we enjoyed sightseeing together. For Ian's twenty-eighth birthday, we took an overnight trip along the Icefields Parkway between Banff and Jasper. We stopped frequently on our first day as we travelled north so our return trip would take less time. We saw the blue glacier snow at the Columbia Icefields, amazing, indescribable views of mountains, valleys, shimmering aspens and waterfalls! We rested our senses for a bit as we walked along a wooded path from the parking lot to the Sunwapta Falls. Being among the trees with a canopy of golden leaves overhead was peaceful and calm and a favourite moment for me. Just because we had to, we visited Lake Annette near Jasper, where we saw moose and elk.

Our last day started with a tram ride up Whistler's Mountain in Jasper. Even though it was quite snowy and the visibility wasn't good for hiking at the top, the views of down below from "way up there" were amazing. On our return trip, because of the snow, everything we had passed the day before looked very different. We had frequent stops again.

Our main stop was at Peyto Lake at the highest point of the parkway. The lake looked especially blue surrounded by white snow. I was very glad that Ian and I had the opportunity to enjoy this trip together, two adults sharing a great experience.

When I moved to Calgary, I hoped to experience the drive west through the mountains sometime. I planned for that trip to include a visit with my niece Marie and her family in Surrey, BC. September 2009 was when the adventure happened! Marie and Matthew had three children, so I decided to stay in a hotel so I'd get more rest before my drive back to Calgary.

I travelled over two days as I planned to stop to read tourism plaques and visit some popular sites along the way. After leaving Calgary, the landscape changed from foothills to mountains as I approached the Rockies. On our trip west in 1986, our family had driven on several treacherous sections of highway. Some of them remained, but there were many improvements. There was a majestic new bridge, supported by five piers, over the steep Kicking Horse Canyon. At the rest stop there I saw majestic mountains and a river with a railroad running alongside it. The railroad was my "companion" for most of my trip.

When the Rockies were behind me, I was soon travelling beside Shuswap Lake. I was interested in seeing this area because my landlord vacationed there. As I approached Kamloops, the landscape reminded me a lot of Honduras, with the same kind of rounded hills with few trees. There was a huge difference in the buildings that were built on those hills, though. From Kamloops, I continued taking the Trans-Canada Highway, driving beside the Thompson River. I enjoyed beautiful, peaceful scenery with the canyon, the flowing river, and the occasional train.

The afternoon of my arrival, I visited Marie for tea. I had a bit of difficulty finding their home but knew I was close by when I found the school Matthew taught at. Two days later, I spent the afternoon at their home and had supper with them. Marie had a busy household, but it was fun and welcoming. There was great teamwork between Matthew and Marie as they managed the busyness of their young family.

In March, when I had started corresponding with Max from Surrey, I had considered his profile because I thought there might be a chance we could meet someday. I did get that opportunity, and Max offered to give me a tour of the area during my visit. I met him the evening of my arrival. We missed seeing a sunset at Crescent Beach but enjoyed a walk along the promenade in White Rock, and we made plans to meet again the next day.

The Tour by Max was quite extensive, including China Town, mountains, water, bridges, awesome views, harbours, and more. The most challenging part of my day was eating dim sum. It wasn't the taste of the food I didn't like but the texture. I hid my discomfort the best I could and ate more of the items I could enjoy. We ended our day watching a beautiful sunset at Britannia Beach. Max was a great tour guide, and he liked showing others "his world."

On my own, I discovered the Serpentine Fen. There are Ducks Unlimited ponds there, with a path that runs alongside them. It was a beautiful sunny day. As I sat on a bench, I watched a lone duck sitting on a log not too far from the edge of the pond. I felt a deep connection with that duck somehow, and I think that part of me knew then that life would take me to BC. I realized that the mountains no longer made me feel confined but now comforted me. Was it the beginning of God revealing His future plan to me? Ian and Leona were both getting restless and wanting a change in their lives. The next few months could be very interesting, I thought. I was challenged to "be still" and wait for God's direction.

On the way back to Calgary, I stopped in Salmon Arm on Saturday evening and attended church there on Sunday morning. It was a huge surprise when a couple I knew well from Strathroy came into the same pew I was in and sat next to me. We were a bit noisy about how surprised and pleased we were to see each other. It made many people notice and smile. Seeing them made me think back on my feelings at church after my divorce. I realized that since my move being "single again" wasn't an issue at church. I felt more comfortable being "me."

The scenery as I continued on to Calgary was even more beautiful than the scenery on the drive to Surrey. There were so many amazing views as I drove towards Mount Revelstoke, through Golden and Rogers Pass, and saw the western sides of the mountains near Banff. I experienced so much in a week that is seemed like I had been gone much longer. On my return, I told people that driving east towards the Rockies was the best part of my trip. On a later trip from BC to Calgary and back, I felt that driving west towards the mountains was more beautiful. I guess going home is best. It's a blessing to have a place that feels like home!

While we lived in Calgary, Ian, Leona, and I enjoyed spending time with "our western family" whenever we had an opportunity. One year we went to Rocky Mountain House for Christmas with Len's family, and another year we shared a turkey dinner with Jon and his wife. Jon and I surprised Mary with an early sixtieth birthday party at his home when Mary and Ed visited Calgary. It was always good to see any family and friends who came to Calgary too. When I left Ontario, I had been told that I would be surprised who I maintained connections with, and that proved to be true. People were in my life for a reason, a season, or a lifetime.

As I had suspected, the next few months were very interesting for my family. Ian planned to go back to school and selected a sixteen-month program in Ottawa, Ontario. Leona wanted to learn more about music composition and voice and applied to a school in Montreal. When she wasn't accepted, she decided to move to Montreal anyway as she felt there would be more music opportunities for her there. Ian's classes would start in January, and Leona planned to move in April.

Christmas that year was a bittersweet time as we had no idea when we would all be together again. We entered 2010 with many adventures ahead of us. Ian took as many of his belongings as he could in his car. Leona was organizing to have a moving company help with her move. She planned to fly to Montreal and take Shadow, the cat, with her. About the future, I wrote, "I don't anticipate staying in Calgary for long once Ian and Leona are both gone from here. If not in BC, I have no clue yet where I'll go."

I decided to fly to BC for a weekend visit in January to see if that would help me with my decision. Max picked me up from the airport, and he later took me to Matthew and Marie's home. On Saturday, my nephew Josh came for a visit, and I went to Ellie's home for tea. Ellie and I had attended school together years earlier and had recently become Facebook friends. It was fun to reconnect again and to share about our families and other people that we both knew.

On Sunday, I went with Max to Christian Life Assembly (CLA), the church he had told me about in his emails. I enjoyed the service very much. Another highlight of the day came later when we saw some eagles. Eagles had been special to me ever since Dad gave me my eagle carving. I had not had any eagle sightings during my September visit in spite of always being on the lookout for them.

Later, as I flew home, I was no nearer to making a decision about whether or not I would move to BC. I still only had that vague feeling I'd had while watching that lone duck sitting on a log. What was the significance of that duck anyway? When I talked to my brother Len, he told me that he and his wife planned to retire in the lower mainland of BC.

After I arrived home, Ellie emailed me to invite me to stay with her family while I looked for housing and a job if I wanted to move to the Surrey area. This was a big decision to make. This wasn't about anyone else; it was only about me. I prayed that God would direct my steps.

On February 10, I wrote, "I am now quite certain I will be moving further west to BC. Ian and Leona are accepting of the idea. It may only be for a season. I had never planned for my time west to be so short; further adventure west seems to be where God is leading. Going back to Ontario would be moving backwards, and that idea makes me feel sad. I will stay in Calgary until Leona leaves." Moving backwards didn't seem right. My decision was made. I would stay with Ellie and her family until I got a job and a place to stay.

———

Before moving, I decided it was time to sort through my photos and make albums for Ian and Leona. I also made scrapbooks with their school-day treasures and keepsakes. In each of their scrapbooks, I had a page of their school photos. When I looked at Leona's photos in chronological order, I could see that she looked sadder with each year. I didn't notice it so much with Ian's pictures, but recently his wife told me that she could see the same thing in his photos. I cannot undo the past.

I was blessed by this quote:

God is in our lives. He is at work right now, undoing Satan's destructive messes and leading us to places he wants us to go. This is true in everything we do and everywhere we go. The key is for us to seek his purpose, to live his will. If that is our goal, then we can be sure our God is with us every step of our way.[6]

———

I made one final trip to Ontario before leaving for BC. I flew into Ottawa to visit Ian and see where he lived and went to school. Together we visited with some family and spent special time with Mom, who was glad to see both of us. I'm thankful we had that visit. As Mom's dementia progressed, she was no longer able to recognize her grandchildren, and due to circumstances beyond my control, I wasn't able to visit Ontario later in the year.

Soon I was leaving my position in residential care. My job had been a bit of a disappointment in some respects. I had not learned as much as I would have liked to, because all of us who worked the evening shift were new staff. However, it was hard to leave the residents, who had dementia. It wasn't really possible to say goodbye to them. I would just disappear from their lives. Who would make business deals with Harold and Ed? Who would reassure Mary and say, "Yes, I remember who you are, and I will come to your party"? Who would tuck Harry into bed at night? The smiles of recognition I received from the residents as I went about my work meant a lot to me. It reminded me that they might not be able to remember what I said or what I did, but they were aware of how I made them feel.

After Leona flew east, I was preparing to drive west. It didn't feel wrong, but it was a bit unsettling. Where would our lives take us? I didn't think about the fact that I was moving across the mountains without a job or my own place to live. When I had moved to Calgary, I had secured a job well in advance and had rented an apartment before arriving there.

---

6 Phil Ware, "Heartlight Daily Verse 3/13," Christianity.com, http://www.christianity.com/devotionals/heartlight-daily-verse-phil-ware/heartlight-daily-verse-3-or-13-557778.html

Somehow I knew that it would all work out. I trusted that God was in control of this very different situation too. After my things were picked up by the movers on April 26, I spent the night with my friend Janet, who worked at Bow-Crest.

Before leaving for BC the next day, I went back to clean the apartment. On some level, my time in Calgary had been a clean-up phase of my life. I developed new and different relationships with my adult children, and I transitioned further into a life that had room for me, for God's plans for *me*.

It was a very foggy day when I left Calgary. Visibility was affected all that afternoon as I drove towards my overnight stop in Salmon Arm, BC. My world was shrouded in mist. I couldn't see the tops of the mountains or too far ahead of me. It was a picture of my life. I felt safe, secure, and cocooned by God's love. It would be a fresh start, a great adventure with God!

chapter fifteen

IN BRITISH COLUMBIA

The grace to let go and let God be God flows from trust in His boundless love.[7]

April 28 was Transition Day for me. In 2008, Mary and I had left Strathroy, Ontario, for my move to Alberta, and two years later, on the same date, I arrived in BC. It was great that I was invited to stay with Ellie's family in Langley. Ellie wasn't going to be home until the evening on the day of my arrival, so I planned to visit with Max while I waited. When I finally arrived in Surrey, after getting quite lost coming off of Highway 1, Max's first words to me were "Welcome home!" I didn't feel connected to those words. I knew that God had tapestry designs planned for me in BC, but I suspected it might take a while before it felt like home.

My move to BC wasn't as frustrating as my move to Alberta had been. There are many differences from province to province. People who have only lived in one province sometimes didn't understand my confusion. I discovered that changing insurances, driver's documents, and other paperwork was easier in BC as more of it could be done online. By using MapQuest, a map book, and sometimes asking someone, I more easily found places I needed to go to.

---

7 Brennan Manning, The *Ragamuffin Gospel* [Colorado Springs, Colorado: Multnomah Books, 2005], 120

During those first weeks, while Ellie was working I tagged along with Max quite often. I met several of his friends and got acquainted with my new surroundings in a way I wouldn't have been able to on my own. Within three weeks, I had a casual relief full-time position at Surrey Memorial Hospital as a float nurse to medical units. During my job orientation, I was still living in Langley, and on a clear day I saw Mount Baker as I drove home. It was still an awesome, majestic mountain that reminded me of God's great power and constant faithfulness. Any day that is clear enough to see Mount Baker is a good day.

Max helped me with my apartment search, as he knew the neighbourhoods. I had hoped to live close to Marie and her family, but the apartments in her neighbourhood were mostly basement apartments with tiny windows. I found a place I liked, near where Max lived, that was available for the end of May. It was aboveground and very spacious. Max was able to visualize how I could separate the large living area into zones. The room was much cozier that way, as there wasn't a big empty space in the middle of the room. I decided to use the smaller bedroom for myself and keep the very large bedroom for whatever else I might want to do.

As I adjusted to my job, many things about working on a medical unit were familiar. However, I needed to learn how the units functioned, how to contact various people and departments, and how to record what I had done. There was one thing that was a scary difference, but the hospital soon changed its procedure. I had worked in one hospital where doctors' orders that had to be carried out immediately were highlighted in yellow marker by the person who recorded the order. At Surrey Memorial Hospital, highlighting an order in yellow marker meant that something had been discontinued. I was very afraid that I might make a serious mistake if the order was about a medication.

One morning, when I had been at my job for about three months, I wasn't feeling well at work and was sent to the emergency department for assessment. It was determined that my thyroid was the problem. Over the next few weeks, as I continued to miss work, I was twice told to take an increased dose of thyroid medication. When I felt anxious and like I was getting too much medication, I was given an antianxiety medication. Finally, one day, I was quite frightened by how I was feeling. I didn't feel that I should call 911, but I knew I had to settle myself. I filled a bottle with some water and got some trail mix and prepared to go to bed for a while.

Fortunately, Max happened to call right at that time. He took me to a walk-in clinic that was open on that Saturday afternoon. I was given a medication to control my heart rate and was told to return to the original dose of thyroid medication. I had already missed one month of work and was very glad that I would soon have some relief from my symptoms. I had been in panic mode, and it was almost embarrassing how much my body settled down, even before I started the heart medication. However, the next days and weeks proved that I did need the medication temporarily.

It was a difficult time when I was off sick. I had no money coming in. When would I see Mom or Ian or Leona? My life in BC didn't seem to be progressing, as I wasn't meeting new people. I had met several of Max's friends, but I hadn't established close personal connections with them. It was still some time before the arrangements were made for me to gradually return to work, because certain protocols had to be followed,

While I wasn't working, I was determined to keep up some level of activity. Ian came for a visit for a few days between semesters. He and I visited his cousin Josh in Vancouver, and one day we went on a Tour by Max. We also went for a drive to Whistler, stopping a few times along the way. Once or twice I was short of breath, and I had to let Ian do some exploring on his own.

It was fascinating that Ian remembered that he had been at Shannon Falls before. It had been in 1986, when Ian was four years old, when we were in BC for Expo. We had been at Shannon Falls with a family that had three boys who were older than Ian. The boys had been climbing on some rocks at the base of the falls. Ian had watched them closely but didn't quite dare to join them. Now, in 2010, Ian didn't remember the falls. He remembered the rocks the boys had been climbing on.

During my recovery time, Mary and Ed also visited. Once again, my family was fortunate to experience a Tour by Max. Mary and Ed enjoyed touring with a local. They had lots of questions, and Max knew the answers. We went for walks at Serpentine Fen and at Boundary Bay. One of my favourite spots was between the ocean and mountains at Boundary Bay. While taking the medication to control my heart rate, I was able to walk flat distances at a steady pace for quite a while. In God's provision, which is sometimes hard to understand, my health situation allowed me to spend more time with family during their visits.

Being ill for so long was discouraging. I began to question why I was in BC. Had I misunderstood God's plan? I wrote, "Mom would still enjoy having me closer. Praying that God will make things clearer—I need to trust Him." One day soon after, as I was driving home from the grocery store, a song came on the radio. I had to stop, as I was blinded by my tears. The song, "Beautiful" by MercyMe, reminded me that God knew all the questions of my hurting heart. Nothing that was happening in my life was a surprise to Him. I was treasured, sacred, and beautiful in His eyes! I had to trust God to guide my steps. My question wasn't answered, but I was able to trust God for an answer.

Shortly after that day of sadness, I wrote, "I'm *very slowly* getting more involved in the community and at church. I'm hoping to move closer to church in the spring. I'll be joining CLA, a Pentecostal church. I'm being blessed there and am now spending more time in the Word and in prayer." I had visited CLA before my move to BC, and I had to trust that God had prepared me for other situations, too.

In a unique way, God had me experience two events that people in BC sometimes talked about. I had been in Alberta when Mount St. Helens erupted in 1980, and I had been to Expo in 1986. It made those threads in my tapestry more significant than I had imagined at the time. Sometimes God's touch is very gentle and easy to overlook.

Over a five-week period I gradually returned to my casual full-time position, still floating where I was needed. Soon a casual relief three-quarter-time position became available. I would permanently work on the medical unit where I presently worked most of my shifts. I decided that position would suit my needs better. I had started to feel connected with the routines of the unit and would also be working with the same group of nurses, so I could develop some workplace friendships. One of the doctors I occasionally worked with had done his family practice residency at the Strathroy hospital, and it was fun sharing some of our mutual experiences.

One challenge on the unit was the lack of teamwork. One day I was *too* busy. Some of my busyness was because I was helping other nurses throughout the day. Ten minutes before my shift ended, I was carrying two supper trays to the kitchen when a patient's call bell went off. One of the nurses sitting calmly at the desk said, "That's your bell, Annette." I knew then that I had to take care of myself and *my* work first. I couldn't trust that there would be help from others. Also, putting patients in the hallway was an accepted way of dealing with congestion in the hospital. I felt it wasn't fair to the patients, as they had no privacy. It wasn't fair to the nurses either, as we were expected to do our normal night routines while tiptoeing around sleeping people.

Since I wasn't able to go to Ontario for Mom's eighty-eighth birthday, I decided that it would be fun to have a birthday party for her in BC. Marie and her family were happy to join me. We knew that Mom couldn't attend, but that didn't stop us. I made one of Mom's favourite desserts, decorated it with candles, and served it on Mom's dessert dishes. I had pictures of her cycling through my digital picture frame. After supper, we played a tabletop version of shuffleboard that is popular in Dutch circles. It was a fun evening and a fun way to honour the years of Mom's life.

By year's end Leona had decided she didn't want to stay in Montreal. I wrote, "Leona is moving to BC. With Leona coming here, my future here is clearer." I was glad that I was using the smaller bedroom because Leona would be able to use the large bedroom for herself and her belongings. Before the end of the year, Leona and our cat Shadow arrived from Montreal.

However, another big move must have been too much for our dear twelve-and-a-half-year-old friend. He died within forty-eight hours of arriving in BC. During his life, Shadow moved from Ontario to Alberta to Quebec to British Columbia. I remembered the day I told Leona to look at the big squirrel in our backyard. She looked at me to see if I was serious and then said, "Mom! That's not a squirrel; that's Shadow." We laughed as we remembered that day. Shadow hadn't been a part of my life for a while, but Leona missed him very much!

During my first months of living in BC, I usually got a ride to church with Max, as he lived nearby. He also gave a ride to other people along the way. It was good to meet more people. Two of the women who often got a ride with Max had been part of his Alpha group. In January 2011, I took the Alpha course, but I missed a few sessions because of work. I learned about the program and I got to know more people. Soon I was recognizing people when entering and leaving the church.

In February 2011, Ian came for a visit. It had been more than a year since I'd had my family of three together. Ian talked a bit about his friendship with an East Indian girl named Manpreet and about where he might live once he was done school. He hoped to live somewhere with four distinct season. While we were exploring some local attractions, Ian saw people tobogganing on Mount Seymour. He thought he might be able to live

in BC someday too. I enjoyed sharing life with both of my children for
a few days. .

———————

One morning when I came home after working a night shift, I saw a
disturbing scene on the patio in front of my apartment door—a stove, refrigerator, microwave, and a few other items that had all obviously been
in a fire. I found out that there had been a fire in the kitchen above my
apartment. The owner's son had left oil on the stove and forgotten about
it when he went to play video games. Previously the son had a very noisy
party with lots of drinking in which his guests had thrown glass bottles
around. I knew it was time for me to find somewhere else to live.

Before Leona started her job at a camp on one of the islands in
Howe Sound, she helped me find another apartment. I decided to try the
Cloverdale area near Marie's home again. This time I was successful in
finding a two-bedroom place that was above ground. It had big windows
in the living spaces and a great outdoor area. I thought the apartment was
too small, but Leona felt that the space would be perfect for me. It would
be a cozy place when I was there alone, but I could have ten people over
for dinner if I wanted to. The location was a less-than-ten-minute walk
from Marie's home and a less-than-fifteen-minute drive from church unless the traffic was heavy.

Once again I had to do a lot of measuring to see what I had room
for and where I would put things. One of the women who got a ride to
church with Max needed some furniture, and I was able to give her some
pieces I no longer needed. Initially Leona's things had to be at my place as
well. My new landlord said we could store some of Leona's belongings in
the garage until she found a place of her own. I could visualize how the
apartment would look once Leona had her own apartment, but initially
it felt a bit cluttered and disorganized. When Leona started working on
the island, she wasn't home often. There was enough room for one person to live comfortably.

Even though the change was good, I had a period of adjustment. Soon I was enjoying my new surroundings. I felt safe walking alone in my new neighbourhood. When I walked to a nearby cemetery on a clear day, I could see mountains in three directions. There was often a lot of activity in the backyard: squirrels jumping from tree to tree and lots of twittering birds. The Steller's jays were just as noisy as the blue jays I was used to in Ontario, but they had a much richer blue colouring.

In the summer, I visited Leona's island for a few days. I had never purposefully gone away to spend a few days with God before. I felt calm and relaxed walking or sitting by the water and seeing the mountains nearby. I had recently bought a book about breaking free from guilt, anger, greed, and jealousy. I hadn't realized how much those emotions were affecting my life. By reading the book and spending time in God's Word and lots of personal reflection, I was able to experience more peace. This became my prayer:

> God, I am so tired of trying to live without You. I come today, desperately longing for You and seeking Your presence. Right now, I surrender to You, giving everything I know about my-self to everything I know about You. Thank You for meeting me at my point of need.[8]

An extra-long water taxi ride back to the mainland was a great way to end my island time.

When Leona had a week off in August, she and I went hiking on Mount Baker in Washington State. We planned to drive to a viewpoint first, but the road was closed because it was still snow-covered. We then

---

8 Mary Southerland, "Come and Rest in Him," Girlfriends in God, March 11, 2016, http://girlfriendsingod.com/come-and-rest-in-him

hiked part of the Heliotrope Ridge Trail. It's a popular trail that starts in a forest and climbs quite steadily to more rocky areas. The water in the creeks we had to cross was quite deep and cold. The first crossing wasn't too bad; the second was more difficult. Even though I enjoyed seeing the wildflowers and waterfalls along the way, I wasn't sure I wanted to go farther.

When we got to the third crossing, Leona offered to continue on alone for a wee bit. I stayed behind. There were several other hikers on the trail, so I had no concerns. A couple coming down told me I needed to go a bit farther or I would regret it. Just past the third crossing I could see a glacier and views of Mount Baker. Wow! I had reached our goal! That mountain was just as hard to climb down as Castle Mountain in Alberta had been. I was very stiff the next day, but it was worth it. It's much easier to see Mount Baker from Surrey on a clear day than to do all that climbing, though.

Recovery Church, which meets at CLA's Langley campus, is a place for addicts, ex-addicts, and others to worship and grow in their relationship with a life-changing God. When I first lived in BC, I attended occasionally. Around the same time, I was assigned to care for addicts at the hospital more often. They were usually being treated for serious infections that required intravenous antibiotics. Nurses often treated them with little respect, and they didn't respect the nurses either. These patients often congregated near the elevators with their friends, and it felt good whenever I heard a "Goodbye, Annette" from one of them as I left my shift.

After my move, I began to attend Recovery Church more regularly. I could relate to people who had chains from their past that needed to be broken. I went to their monthly Saturday morning prayer meetings and was asked to be on the prayer team. I was blessed when I realized that God was using lessons I had learned and was still learning through my personal struggles.

When Ian was finished school in Ottawa, he decided to move to BC as well. His friend Manpreet also came. It seemed good that they were coming to Surrey, which has a large East Indian community. They arrived at the beginning of September. On her first outings, Manpreet wanted to see places by the ocean. When we went to the pier at White Rock Beach, she especially enjoyed watching the starfish.

I was sharing my apartment with Ian and Manpreet, and when Leona finished her job on the island, she was there too. Losing my privacy made it difficult for me to deal with the situation. We didn't communicate well enough to create routines that might have helped the situation.

One day when I needed to talk about my frustrations, I went for a walk with Max. He was an encouraging, affirming friend who wasn't afraid to challenge me towards personal growth. I told him that my frustrations made me behave badly. It was good to say out loud some of the things I had been keeping hidden inside. I needed to remember that God loved my family and me and that I could trust Him and His plans for the future.

Sometimes God's mysterious ways are beyond my understanding. I wasn't proud of my strong reactions, but it seemed a bit positive that I was reacting rather than absorbing all my feelings. Now I needed to learn how to control my reactions. Prayers continued for all of us. God's answers did not come quickly as I understand "quickly."

It was good that I had already planned to go away for a while. I spent a week in Ontario at the end of October so I would be there for Mom's eighty-ninth birthday. Mary and I spent time together planning a small birthday party for Mom in an activity room at Shalom Manor. We served tea using Mom's teacups and teapot. We celebrated with a few of Mom's friends, five children, including in-laws, five grandchildren, and five great-grandchildren. Mom enjoyed it when we sat with her for one-on-one visits.

Mom's dementia was a bit more pronounced, but I still felt like I had a visit with my mother. I felt loved and cared about. Mom often mentioned that Clarence was taking care of her money, but I don't think she realized how much Mary did for her. I was blessed knowing that Mary and Clarence were there for Mom. While in Ontario I also had a chance to meet Clarence's grandson. Aiden was born with chronic kidney disease, and he, his parents, and his grandparents were often in my thoughts and prayers.

———

It had been good to be away. I returned home to a living situation that continued to be challenging. I felt badly that we didn't feel more unity among us and there were a lot of hurt feelings. It was too hard for four adults to adjust to living together in such a small space. In time, Ian and Manpreet found a place of their own. On Christmas Day, Ian, Leona, and I had dinner together, but Manpreet had other plans. Later that week, when I had a birthday dinner for Max, Ian and Manpreet were there too. Max was a friend to all of us.

———

I was working in a part-time relief line at the hospital, even though I was still officially a casual employee. I wasn't able to control when I worked and still wasn't able to get involved in things at church in a way I would have liked to. After talking with the scheduling clerk at work, I took a bold step and stopped doing relief positions. I only picked up casual shifts, usually shifts that were available because of full-time nurses' vacations. I seldom had to take shifts at the last minute, as I usually got enough booked shifts. These were still twelve-hour shifts, both day and night shifts. However, it wasn't long before I stopped picking up any night shifts.

Picking my own shifts worked well for me. I wanted and needed a more stable routine for myself. It was good to feel more in control of my life. I was able to be a table leader for Alpha and an usher every other month in the morning service at CLA. I began giving people rides to Recovery Church. One of those trips was filled with laughter as my rider and I shared our knowledge of the importance of not whistling in prison. She said, "Some people don't know that." The importance of where we had been diminished as friendships were formed. Where we were going became more important. For the first time I attended Recovery Church baptisms at Derby Reach, where people were baptized in the Fraser River.

In February, Leona went on a trip to Italy, and soon after her return she moved into her own apartment. During the off-season from her job on the island, Leona worked in Langley. Through the store where she worked, she was able to buy some furniture she liked very much. When moving day came, Max helped us move many of her bigger items. It was good to see Leona have a new beginning. Her apartment was about a fifteen-minute drive from where I lived. Ian and Manpreet still lived locally too.

Clarence and Jeri's grandson Aiden was now on peritoneal dialysis, and it was a busy time for them as they supported their daughter and her family. Jeri visited me for a weekend when she came to congratulate her newlywed friends who lived in BC. We had a full weekend of activities. We went to the Skagit Valley Tulip Festival in Washington State and visited her friends in Horseshoe Bay and Whistler and our niece Marie. Jeri appreciated the weekend away and the distraction of doing something totally different for a few days. I had great "sisters' time" with her and also enjoyed exploring some new places.

At the end of May I went to visit my nephew Jon and his family in Calgary. When we were on an outing to Heritage Park, Jon asked if I would like to take his three-year-old son Jonah for his first Ferris wheel ride. I don't like rides much, but I agreed to the adventure, and Jon decided to come with us. We got settled in for our ride and didn't say much initially. When our seat got to the top and we were swinging a bit, Jon said, "I don't like this too much." I admitted that I didn't either. Then Jonah said he wanted down. Jon told Jonah that he was going to get his first lesson in commitment. We had to complete what we had set out to do. Soon, Jonah was saying "Weeeee" and enjoying the ride. My nephew and grandnephew were lucky that this old auntie was ready for an adventure that day.

I had thoroughly enjoyed my time spent with members of my extended family over recent weeks. Even though I usually felt confident that I was where I was meant to be, I still sometimes struggled with a sense of direction for my life. One day when I feeling lost and alone, I was walking around in a drugstore waiting for a prescription to be filled. I asked God to show me that He cared about me in a real way. I began looking at greeting cards and noticed a sixtieth birthday card. The message was "In sixty years you can touch a lot of lives, you can share a lot of wisdom, and you can bring a lot of joy—if you're someone as special as you, that is." I knew then that it was time to start writing my story. I would use my sixtieth birthday as the ending point.

For most of my life I had saved mementoes of various events. I had two small bins full of old cards, reports, and calendars, plus the journals I had written following the end of my marriage. I began my book project by reviewing the contents of my bins. Dad had written his autobiography to share with his family, but I felt that my story might have a larger audience. It was a challenge to leave out some of the extended family stories, but by making revisions, a story emerged about things that had affected me and my life.

In the summer, I leisurely dabbled at working on my book project while I took a twelve-day staycation. I went out each day and explored some of the tourist attractions in my new world, BC. One day I included Marie and her children when I went for a long walk at a park I hadn't explored yet. I went to Stanley Park with Ian and walked in Green Timbers Park, where Leona often ran. I left the TV off, ate as many meals as I could outdoors, and posted photos on Facebook. It was fun to share my adventures with my family and friends, and it was good to spend some time doing these things for "me."

One of the craziest outings that summer was blackberry picking with Max. Blackberry bushes with all their brambles grew wildly along many of the ditches and fences. The berries were delicious, but picking them was a scratchy job, so I wore long pants, a long-sleeve shirt, and shoes. Max bought a plank that we could throw across the ditches so we would be able to reach the bounty on the other side. It was a great idea—except that I had a misstep shortly after we started. I slipped beside the plank and went waist-deep into the water in the ditch. I was laughing as I climbed back onto the plank, but I was soaking wet. Fortunately, the water wasn't as murky as it looked. It was a warm day, and even though I was very wet for a while, we were able to pick as many berries as we wanted. I earned the name "Blackberry Queen" that day.

———

When I got more focused on writing, I decided that I would work through the tough stuff first: the years during and immediately after my marriage. I didn't realize then how powerfully working through the events of those years would affect me. Doing research for my book was an emotional, often tiring, experience. I tried to be extra careful to take care of myself. I started going for a walk every morning; it was a good way to start the day and helped me lose some weight as well.

As the days grew shorter and the mornings were darker, my thoughts became darker too. The feelings of guilt and shame I had experienced previously returned. Again and again, I fell into the enemy's trap and was robbed of my joy, even though I wasn't really sure what I felt guilty about or what I was ashamed of. I wondered, had I really given what I needed to give to the situation? In many ways, Bob had been an absentee husband, but had I fought for my marriage, or had I allowed it to deteriorate? Then I remembered that, after the end of our marriage, I found Bob's profile on a singles site. Most of the good things he mentioned about his life had happened during our marriage. There was something healing about that.

Another morning, those undefinable negative feelings came upon me once again. Immediately, for a brief moment, a light shone in the sky. I'm not sure what that light was, but God had often reminded me of His love for me through glimpses of sunlight. That light was a statement for me. God also lovingly and graciously reminded me of the times He would whisper to my heart words of Jeremiah 31:3: "I have loved you with an everlasting love."

I still remember where I was sitting the day I found a paper with two questions that I had written years earlier. I finally had to confront two deep-rooted fears. *Am I capable of being a good parent? Am I lovable enough for remarriage?* Tears flowed as I admitted to myself that those feelings were still present in my life. There was a deep cleansing that day when I remembered conversations that had taken place twenty-five years earlier during marriage counselling sessions with Keith and Patsy.

I will rewrite a few lines from 1986:

In that discussion, we talked about my "nursing personality." As a student nurse, I had been praised for my ability to deal with a sad situation in one room and switch to a happy situation in the next room. During counselling sessions I was told that most people can't switch their feelings that easily. My "quick switch" could make Bob feel like I didn't care or I was ignoring his feelings.

Also from 1986:

Some sessions were brutally difficult for me. There seemed to be a lot of extra support for Bob. I felt confused and hurt and more negative about myself than I ever had. Later, Keith explained to me that he had used that approach so Bob would continue coming for further sessions.

Unfortunately, during our counselling sessions I hadn't been able to sort through which comments were real and which ones were made to keep Bob attending sessions. I had just been through six difficult years of marriage. I survived during the next eleven years of marriage, but I didn't thrive. Those confused, hurt, and negative feelings about me were never dealt with. For years I had wondered if I was capable of caring, and it had affected my relationship with Bob and my children.

Am I capable of being a good parent? Am I lovable enough for remarriage? Praise the Lord, after twenty-five years I recognized that those questions didn't come from a loving Father. First, I realized that the comments about my nursing personality didn't make sense. As a nurse, I switched my emotions in two different situations, not with the same person. In reality, people may have benefited from my ability to be affected by Bob yet carry on with the rest of my life as though all was well. God had showed me again and again that I didn't need to walk with guilt or shame. I had felt Him lift my head, and I had seen the sunshine of His love. I praised God for the healing work He was doing in my life, and I began to recognize that He had been present in all our lives. God was and continues to be the healer and restorer in my children's lives.

However, I had to deal with my anger and grief. I had questioned my ability to properly parent my children for so long because of the discussions we had. I have been able to forgive Keith and Patsy for their counselling methods, which I feel failed me as a person, and my children, too. I remembered that Keith had tried to connect with Bob on his own, but that had failed. I remembered that Keith and Patsy had referred me to the lawyer who had helped me through my divorce. God's ways are mysterious. God is God, and He is love! The threads of my tapestry sometimes have patterns that are dark and jagged but then become bright, shiny, and smooth.

In time, it became easier for me to accept the need to take care of myself, mind, body, and spirit. I often think about the instructions the flight attendants give about the oxygen mask before an airplane takes off. If you are travelling with a child or someone who requires assistance, put your mask on first, and then assist the other person. It was an important life lesson for me to learn. God's plan is for me to allow God to help me so I can help others. "Praise be to the God and Father of our Lord Jesus Christ, the Father of compassion and the God of all comfort, who comforts us in all of our troubles, so that we can comfort those in any trouble with the comfort we ourselves have received from God" (2 Corinthians 1:3–4).

In late October 2012, I flew to Ontario for Mom's ninetieth birthday celebration. Ed, Mary, Clarence, Jeri, Len, and I had lunch with her in the activity room of the facility where she lives. She enjoyed seeing all the familiar faces around the table. On the Saturday following her birthday, we had an open house for selected guests, which included the immediate family and my cousins. Mom's dementia had advanced, and I think she was a bit overwhelmed by so many faces and the busyness around her. She had always been a very gracious hostess, and she was on that day, too. It was great to see her core personality shine through.

A few months before my fifty-ninth birthday a representative from the Hospitals of Ontario Pension Plan called me. She said, "You're not going to wait until you're sixty before you start collecting your pension, are you?" I hadn't given any thought into collecting earlier, but I decided that researching the subject might be worthwhile. I found out that because I was no longer contributing to the plan, it would be beneficial for me to start getting monthly benefits early. I could continue to work and save the pension money I got. I appreciated that I would have a steady monthly income apart from my casual employment. I made arrangements to start collecting my hospital pension at the age of fifty-nine. It was a good feeling.

Since Christmas 1983 the holiday season had usually been a bit exhausting for me. I had to work my assigned shifts but tried to attend special events and family functions and make the season festive at home, too. In 2012, twenty-nine years later, I didn't have an assigned schedule. I limited the number of shifts I worked so that I was able to celebrate the reason for the season and attend events at church. I spent one Sunday afternoon lying on the loveseat listening to Christmas carols, something I had wanted to do every year but seldom found time for.

When I had moved to the neighbourhood, I had smiled when I noticed that this girl with a Dutch-Reformed background had moved from an area where most of my neighbours were Punjabi to a neighbourhood with two Reformed churches. On Christmas Eve, I attended a candlelight service at the Canadian Reformed Church, complete with choir and orchestra. It was beautifully done. On Christmas morning, I attended a service at the United Reformed Church. At the end of it, we sang "Ere zij God" ("Glory to God"). This hymn had been a part of my Christmas Day celebration many times during my life. Some people were singing the Dutch version and others were singing the English version at the same time. It's a true cacophony of praise!

The Christmas celebrations continued. Leona came in the afternoon, and later Ian and Manpreet arrived in their Santa hats. My family of four was able to have Christmas dinner together and then open our gifts. On December 29, Marie and her family, Josh and his wife, and Leona came for dinner. It was great to have ten people sitting around the table that had once belonged to Dad and Mom. Mom would have been pleased! I had enough energy to enjoy it all. God was so faithfully teaching me and showing me ways of caring for myself.

———

As I approached my fifty-ninth birthday, I remembered a time after the end of my marriage when I felt like God was saying to me, "It's time to get out of the nest, Annette. It's time to fly!" I was taking better care of myself, so where and what did God want me to do? My questioning mind heard the song "Home" sung by Phillip Phillips.[9] It includes the words "I'm going to make this place your home." I felt God saying to me, "Annette, you're *here* because of you, because of the things I have *here* for you. I love *you* enough to plan this for *you!*" God had a purpose and a plan for me in BC. I had to trust Him and His timing.

---

9 Andrew Pearson, Greg Holden, "Home," copyright Warner/Chappell Music, Inc., Cypmp

Working twelve-hour shifts was becoming too challenging for me. I often felt like I was getting over the flu when I came home from work, very tired and aching all over. I knew that it wasn't good for my body or emotional health to continue in this way. Also, nursing had changed very much over the years. I was no longer able to have the connections with patients that I once enjoyed. I thought I might have to look for something different. I decided that before I left the nursing profession completely, I'd see if home health care might be a possibility.

During my interview, I was warned that switching from hospital nursing to community nursing would be different. "Different" was the exact word I was looking for. I had never considered working in home health care before, as I felt certain that I wanted to have another nurse to discuss my concerns with. However, I had become aware that, more and more, other nurses were coming to me with their questions. I should be able to go solo.

During my two and a half years on medical units in BC, my manager had encouraged me to be a mentor to younger nurses. I thanked him for that when I realized that those situations had helped prepare me for the change I was about to make. My manager was a Christian, and I told him how God had been directing my path. I had been very tired and frustrated at times during my hospital shifts. However, those threads in my tapestry had not been a mistake. God had been preparing me for something different. I was still in nursing, the profession that had been a blessing to me for years in many ways.

From mid-March until April 19, except for a few preplanned days off, I was on a full-time home-health orientation. There was much more for me to learn than I had anticipated. Most nurses at the office were very helpful, and that helped make the transition easier. My past experiences in nursing were helpful, but it was humbling to go from being an experienced nurse in the hospital to a novice nurse in the community.

During my weeks of orientation, Ian called me to let me know that he and Manpreet were going to take two big steps in their lives. They were both going to be baptized, and they were planning to be married soon. I told Ian that I was proud of him for planning to take these steps. He and Manpreet were baptized in a Baptist church they were attending, and that was where their wedding would be, too. Five weeks before the date, Ian and Manpreet decided to get married on May 11. Several women from their church helped Manpreet with wedding planning, though she had several ideas of her own, too. Much of the food was catered in, but Leona made lasagnas, vegetable trays, and trays of sweets for the wedding reception too. I helped Leona as I was able, purchased some supplies that were needed, and prepared for the arrival of family coming for the wedding. It was a busy time as I had just completed my orientation and was still adjusting to my new job.

When Ian told me that Bob was coming to the wedding, I knew it was the right time for Ian and Leona to see him again. It had been a few years since Bob had seen either of his children. It was good for Ian and Leona to have an opportunity to develop relationships with Bob as the adults they now were. It was the right time for me, too. I was no longer running away from the past but was becoming more firmly planted in the life God had for me now. Bob will always be a part of my life as the father of my children. I didn't want to prevent any blessings that could develop in their relationships and prayed that positive things would happen.

The day before the wedding May 10, 2013, was Leona's thirtieth birthday. Her day was almost completely overshadowed by wedding busyness. However, Leona and I took time away from the chaos of preparations to go out for lunch together. For me, it definitely was a day worth celebrating.

I appreciated that some of Ian's uncles and aunts from Ontario and Alberta and his cousin Ryan from Iowa came to the wedding on such short notice. Manpreet's family was still in India and did not attend, so the presence of Ian's family was especially appreciated. Before the wedding, I also started preparations for lunch on Sunday. I invited Bob to join my local and out-of-town family, too. There would be a total of fourteen people present then.

Ian and Manpreet's wedding was on May 11, 2013. Ian and Manpreet asked Max to walk Manpreet down the aisle and to be master of ceremonies at their reception. Leona attended as Ian's "best person," wearing a long-sleeved black sweater over her lovely green dress. The ceremony was performed by the same pastor who had baptized Ian and Manpreet a few weeks earlier and was very meaningful. At the reception, Manpreet was a gracious hostess, and Max made the guests feel comfortable and welcome. There was much laughter and many smiling faces. It was good to hear that there were very few things that Ian and Manpreet would have changed about the day. I was very glad that it had been a good day for them and the earlier busyness hadn't spoiled the day.

Over the summer, I adjusted to my new job and was enjoying it more and more. It was the "different" I had been looking for. I had more time to give clients emotional support and to do health teaching. Besides dealing with more acute-care needs, home health involved doing palliative care in people's homes, making sure they were supported by the resources they needed during this challenging time. It was good to see how comfortable many families were in caring for someone who wished to die at home. It was an honour and a privilege to be part of their team.

After being so stressed and working so hard in the hospital, it seemed like a bonus that my pay rate was the same—I hadn't really thought about this when applying for the job. There was another bonus as well. All the time I had worked in Surrey Memorial Hospital, I had been a casual employee, covering for positions that were vacant because of illness. When I started at home health, I was still working for the Fraser Health Authority. I had worked many hours as a casual employee, so I was close to the top of the casual seniority list. This was great when picking which shifts I wanted to work. A gold star on my tapestry!

———

In early August, I went to Ontario for a visit, as Len was in Ontario too so he could officiate at a wedding. This gave my three siblings and me an opportunity to spend an evening together. With four of us living in three provinces, it took a bit of coordination to make sibling gatherings happen. A highlight of my visit was attending the wedding of one of my friends. We had maintained our friendship since Divorce Care days, and it was wonderful that my visit to Ontario happened on the weekend of her wedding!

On this visit, I rented a car, which was a new experience for me. I missed some of the opportunity for conversations while driving, but I enjoyed the experience of travelling the roads I had travelled alone before. It was good to realize that I had enjoyed those "alone" times more than I had acknowledged to myself.

After I moved from Strathroy, Mary gave me updates on my grade-school friend Helen, who had MS. I visited Helen for the last time when Mary went to feed her. I wrote, "As I saw all the disabilities she must deal with every day of her life, I was reminded of a conversation we had many years ago. She told me then that she wasn't afraid to die but was challenged by what she might have to go through until the day of complete healing. As I now remember the look of peace on her face when I visited with her so recently, I am amazed and blessed to know how powerful God's presence in our lives can be. She has difficulty seeing, swallowing, and speaking and is unable to move her arms or feet, yet her eyes shine with peace. Awesome God! There is a huge lesson in that for me as I live my life." "I sought the LORD, and he answered me; he delivered me from all my fears. Those who look to him are radiant" (Psalm 34:4–5). Helen died on February 6, 2015.

Later, Mary and I went for a trip down memory lane. Our first stop was a cemetery in Forest, Ontario, with lots of familiar names, of people who had gone to the Forest church and people I had cared for in the hospital in Strathroy. We had an opportunity to tour the Forest church we had attended, which had few changes, except it was now used as flea market. Later we drove past the farms where we lived during those early years. Several of the names on the mailboxes were still familiar, though I'm quite certain the people living there were from a different generation.

When we drove by Hydes' fruit farm, I remembered one year when we picked sour cherries. At least one of us ended up doubled up on the car floor with belly pains (no seat belts in those days). In Sarnia, we spent a bit of time at the Bluewater Bridge before driving past familiar homes and schools on our way back to Strathroy. It was great to share all the memories with my sister, who had lived through most of the same experiences I had in those early years.

Before I returned to BC, Mary and I went to visit Mom at Shalom Manor in Grimsby. I drove the car I had rented and parked it in a spot close to the front door. As we were walking into the building, Mary noticed something strange and said, "Annette, what's wrong with your car?" By the time I turned around, the steam had turned into black smoke. Soon flames were shooting out from under the hood. It was an incredibly helpless feeling.

Events happened quickly. Someone called 911, a taxi appeared, and the driver used his fire extinguisher on the car. When the fire marshal appeared, he told me the fire wasn't my fault. Through all of this, the fire alarm was tolling throughout the seniors' facility, and there was quite an audience. Sometime in all this mayhem, two men appeared in a white truck, got the fire hose out of the seniors' complex, and sprayed down the cars that were parked beside my car. They disappeared as quickly as they had appeared, and no one knew who they were. Angels?? There were a lot of people there who thought that was true.

After the fire was out, I had to call the rental company and arrange for another car. The fire had mostly been contained under the hood, but everything under there was a melted mess. It was still possible to see the shape of the battery and the spout for adding oil to the car. Mary went to visit Mom, who came to see the disaster that had befallen the car. It wasn't often that Mom would walk that far, so it was one good thing in the whole situation.

Thinking about the "what ifs" was a mistake, and I managed not to until the tow truck driver arrived with the new rental vehicle. He needed to unload the new car and then load up the burned-out car. While he worked, he told us stories that I would rather not have heard. We were safe, God had protected us with His timing, and now we had a way to get back to Mary's home. The replacement car had many fancy features, too many for me to sort out in my frazzled state. As we were driving, Mary suddenly began to laugh. "Annette, is your bum warm? You have your seat warmer on," she said. It was funny and maybe a good thing that I hadn't noticed the heat yet.

I had brought with me two CDs that I used to play often while driving Ian and Leona to and from school. I wanted to experience driving and having that worship time again. It was interesting to listen to those same songs several years later and realize how the words had impacted my life. After the car fire I was unable to remove one of the CDs from the CD player. Of the two CDs, the one that was left in the car was the easiest to replace. It was good to be reminded that the fire was no surprise to God!

————

Living in BC, I saw Len and his family more frequently. Marie lived close by, and I enjoyed any time I was able to be with her and her family. When Len's son Josh got married, Mary was at another wedding, but Clarence came. It wasn't often that "the three little ones" were the only siblings at an event. When Len and Nienke bought a condo in Cloverdale, near Marie's home, it solidified their plans to retire in BC. I look forward to when they are in BC permanently.

Sometimes living in BC felt like being over the mountains and far away. I saw familiar faces at various times in various places, several of which I've already mentioned. Janet, a nurse I had worked with in Calgary, stayed with me twice when she had appointments nearby. Leona and I took my niece Elisa, from Moose Jaw, out for lunch when she had a seminar to attend in Vancouver. Clarence took me out for supper when he was in town on business. And even though Ellie lived locally, she was like a visitor from my past because of our shared history. However, I still missed the relationships I had with my Divorce Care and YaYa friends. I missed the way we shared challenges and victories, corrected each other, and experienced lots of laughter.

During the years that I had been in BC, I had occasionally had brief conversations with a woman named Diane. I always enjoyed those times. One day that fall, we decided that we would meet for coffee at her home to get to know each other better. I arrived around 10 a.m., and after 3:30 p.m. we both realized that we were hungry. We had totally lost track of the time. I was very blessed by that time of sharing, praying, laughing, and crying. I gained an awesome sister-friend that day.

———

Becoming a mother-in-law was not easy for me. Max noticed that I had difficulty letting go of my "family of three." I realized that Ian's first loyalty had to be to his wife, but my heart and my head were out of sync. It was a relief when after quite some time Max mentioned that I was do-ing a better job of being more inclusive when talking about Manpreet. I hadn't consciously noticed a shift in my thinking, but I was glad to know that I had made some progress. Challenges continued. Through calm and stormy times, my growth lessons never stopped. I needed to let go and let God be God of my family. He proved Himself faithful so many times and in so many ways.

In November I invited Manpreet out for lunch on her birthday. Le-ona was with me when I picked her up, and Manpreet was glad to see her. Now it felt a bit more like a party. There was another surprise, too, though. When we got to the restaurant, Max was waiting for us. Man-preet appreciated Max's friendship and sometimes teasingly called him "Dad" because he had agreed to walk her down the aisle at her wedding. The birthday surprise was a success!

That year, Ian and Manpreet decided that they would like to have Christmas dinner at their apartment later in the afternoon on Christmas Day. On Christmas morning, I picked Leona up, and we attended a Christ-mas Day service together. After lunch at Leona's apartment, we went for a long walk. We purposefully said "Merry Christmas" to those we passed as we walked. It was fun to get smiles and greetings back and to be recognized by those we passed for a second time. We were hungry and ready for the delicious meal Ian and Manpreet served us before we opened gifts.

While I was doing research for this book, I found Jenny VanDyk's obituary in my box of keepsakes. I noticed that her daughter, Jacqueline, lived in BC, and with the help of the Internet I was able to connect with her. I still had a picture of Mary and me with Jenny that was taken when she helped my mother after my brothers were born. I also found a picture of me in my wedding dress talking to sixteen-year-old Jaqueline. One evening after Christmas, I was invited to join the Van Dyk and Firkin family for dinner. It was a fun reunion for both of us. That thread in my tapestry stretches from my toddler days to my much later adult years in BC—awesome!

Early in 2014, I suddenly had the idea that Leona and I might benefit (mostly financially) from sharing an apartment. I was a bit surprised, but pleased, when she thought it was a great idea. We had several discussions about the kind of place we wanted. We were mother and daughter but also two adults looking for a place to share. Important things on our list were two bedrooms with one large enough for Leona to use as her personal retreat, a kitchen separate from the living area, and an outdoor space. We also needed to decide how to store the "stuff" that we wouldn't need when we combined *two* two-bedroom apartments into *one* two-bedroom apartment.

We looked at several places in different locations. On my sixtieth birthday, we found a place that suited our needs very well. Our new apartment was very close to major transit routes, which was important for Leona, and closer to work but farther from church for me. It had two roomy bedrooms, a large dining-living room combination, a galley kitchen, and a wraparound balcony. One of the best features was its two storage areas. We would be able to store most of our extra belongings in one storage space, and I would be able to use the other one as an office. The apartment was so much better than anything else we had seen, better than anything we had imagined.

On my birthday, I was remembered through Facebook messages, emails, and phone calls from many family members and friends. Towards the end of the day I got an email from Frank, my German pen pal of forty-three years. He and I had never met because he still lived behind the Iron Curtain both times I was in the Netherlands. Now, he and his wife planned to do a tour of Canada at the end of July 2014. They would have two days in Vancouver at the end of the trip and hoped to meet me then. It was the icing on the cake for my special birthday.

For two years, I worked towards finishing my story before I became sixty years old. Some place inside of me had wondered what dramatic ending God would give me.

As I moved forward, I had God's promise that He would help me get better at being the "me" He created me to be. He would lead me forward step by step in His plan for me and those I love. "Yes, my soul, find rest in God; my hope comes from him" (Psalm 62:5).

chapter sixteen
LOOKING BACK

I will instruct you and teach you in the way you should go; I will counsel you with my loving eye on you.

—Psalm 32:8

THROUGH THE YEARS OF MY MARRIAGE, THERE WERE TWO VERSES THAT WERE a special encouragement to me, "Take delight in the LORD, and he will give you the desires of your heart" (Psalm 37:4) and "The light shines in the darkness, and the darkness has not overcome it" (John 1:5). I felt that the light would shine in the darkness and I would have the desires of my heart. Even though life has been different than I anticipated, God has continued to bless me with these verses.

"The light shines in the darkness, and the darkness has not overcome it" (John 1:5). My comfort was in the word *overcome* as it affirmed that darkness cannot defeat the light. In some situations it had been hard to believe that this light would continue to shine. I thank God for the ways He reminded me of His light in the darkness.

Light shone brightly in my darkness when God revealed Himself to me through nature. Again and again God whispered to me that He had an awesome gift for me and that I was worthy of His attention. Many times when I was too tired or discouraged to pick up the Word, God reached out to me through the works of His hands. There is so much variety in nature, so many different birds, plants, and animals with such creative variations. This helped me accept more easily that my life didn't need to look "normal." God could be creative in my situations and in my relationships, too.

God's Word was a lamp unto my feet and a light unto my path. Songs, inspirational quotes, and self-help books were blessings as well. Many times what I read was exactly what my heart needed to hear. As my relationship with the Lord grew, I was able to discern His whispers to my heart, and what a joy that was.

The insights I gained when working through the exercises from the twelve-step program also lightened my darkness. God helped me become a better me, a process that continues to this day. I pray that ongoing growth in these five areas will bless my relationships with my three grown children and others. The Weaver loves me, and I trust Him more and more.

God's light in the world often shines through people. I was blessed by my children, parents, siblings, extended family, church family, and colleagues at work. I enjoyed friendships through my YaYa and UFO groups, Grief Share, Divorce Care, and Alpha. Threads of my tapestry spread farther through my pen pals Frank, Ron, and later Ron's daughter Stacy, who became a loved sister. And Max, a thread that started in Calgary and now connects with me and my family in BC. Lastly, I think of all the "Dutch Bingo" surprises that brought joy into my life at unexpected times and in unexpected places. "Two are better than one, because they have a good return for their labor: If either of them falls down, one can help the other up. But pity anyone who falls and has no one to help them up" (Ecclesiastes 4:9–10).

"Take delight in the LORD, and he will give you the desires of your heart" (Psalm 37:4). For every promise from God, there is an action for me. My assignment in taking delight in the Lord is discovering more about Him and following His will. When I delight in the Lord, He gives me so much more than what I want. He gives me access to His plan through the Holy Spirit's work in my life.

Shortly after I moved to BC, I started attending Recovery Church. I was deeply blessed by the testimonies of the people whose lives had been radically changed. While I was married, I had used poor coping mechanisms and had struggled with the addiction of codependency. I had hurt those I loved by making poor choices about how to care for myself. I had been a poor example of how to live a victorious life. In time I became a part of the prayer team, and God showed me that He could use many of the challenges in my life in a positive way. I was blessed that I understood some of the pain that women who came for prayer were experiencing. I was able to begin to truly believe that with God nothing is wasted.

God was also blessing me in another area of my life. When I started my nursing career, I wanted to be involved with patients and their families. However, I was so busy when I was doing bedside nursing that I no longer enjoyed what I was doing. I had lots of nursing knowledge but was very frustrated. Then, God led me to something different, to home health. I enjoyed the contact with clients in their homes and had time to teach, guide, and support. During the mild winters in BC, I realized that I probably would not have wanted to do home health in the other provinces I had lived in. The anticipation of more snow and colder weather would make the job much less enjoyable.

Looking back, I see painful periods in our life, but I did not go through them alone. In the loneliest times, God was there. In the times when I felt like a failure as a wife, a mother, and a person, God held me. By the end of my marriage, I was broken physically and emotionally. For a long time after that life was too busy for healing happen easily. I am thankful for all the intensely blessed experiences I had while I inched forward with my life.

Changes came more quickly after I moved away from Ontario. I moved to Calgary at the age of fifty-four with a job and a place to live. When my fifty-fifth birthday came, I went on a month's vacation. At the time, I had a place to live but no job. A year later, I moved to BC with no place to live and no job. There were so many transitions in my thinking and so many steps of faith that in hindsight were easily taken. I was moving forward with more confidence.

As I was doing a rewrite of this book, God connected some dots for me. In 2004, after my fiftieth birthday, Pastor Fred preached about Abraham picking up his tent and leaving his country and his father's household. I knew then that it wasn't the right time for me to leave Strathroy. I would need to wait for further direction. During my September 2009 visit to BC, I felt a deep connection with a lone duck sitting on a log at the Serpentine Fen. Somehow, part of me knew then that life would take me to BC. When I was trying to make a decision about moving, I remembered that lone duck. I often wondered, what is the significance of that duck anyway? For several years, I had a framed photo of that duck in my office. Then as I was going through my story once again, God whispered to my heart that the nudge I felt about moving in 2005 was a dot that connected to another dot: that lone duck on the log. God had planned in 2005 for my life to be in BC, in His time.

Trusting the Designer when we see how the dots behind us connect helps us look with more confidence to the dots ahead. Often the connections are obvious, but sometimes they remain hidden from view. All the connected dots help make a beautiful tapestry. This earthly journey is not without adventure. My story continues to unfold in BC with joys and challenges.

chapter seventeen
LOOKING FORWARD

I have felt His hand upon me in great trials and submitted to
His guidance, and I trust that as He shall further open the
way I will be ready to walk therein, relying on His help and
trusting in His goodness and wisdom.[10]

MY FATHER HAD TOLD ME THAT HE DIDN'T THINK I WAS TOO OLD TO BE
transplanted, and God told me that He was going to make "this place"
my home. With God as my centre, I will be a healthy tree in a new and
different way in this place where I am now planted.

As I progress in keeping myself healthy physically, emotionally,
and spiritually, God will spread my roots, and I will become more firmly
planted where God has placed me. "But blessed is the one who trusts in
the LORD, whose confidence is in him. They will be like a tree planted
by the water that sends out its roots by the stream. It does not fear when
heat comes; its leaves are always green. It has no worries in a year of
drought and never fails to bear fruit" (Jeremiah 17:7–8).

———

One day, in my mind and heart I saw two moving pictures from God.

In the first one, an invisible hand was guiding a young boy along a
fishing pier towards a lake. The boy was obediently walking forward but
with fear and trepidation. When the boy got to the end of the pier, he
was brave enough to jump into the lake.

---

10 Abraham Lincoln, *Recollected Words of Abraham Lincoln*, comp. and ed. Don Fehrenbacher and Virginia Fehrenbacher [Stanford, California: Stanford University Press,
1996], 500

In the second picture, I saw the same boy running down the pier, exuberantly, with whoops and hollers. With arms and legs flailing everywhere, he jumped joyously into the lake.

In the next chapter of my life, I want to become more like that second picture, joyfully going where God leads me. *He makes me come alive!*